IN MY FATHER'S FOOTSTEPS

First edition, published in 2001 by

WOODFIELD PUBLISHING
Woodfield House, Babsham Lane, Bognor Regis
West Sussex PO21 5EL, England.

ISBN 1-903953-03-0

In My Father's Footsteps

A *pilgrimage to*
Singapore and Thailand

Patricia Bienkowski

Woodfield Publishing
~WEST SUSSEX • ENGLAND ~

Contents

ACKNOWLEDGEMENTS

'Thanks!' to my husband George for the support and encouragement he gave me with regard to my Pilgrimage and writing this book.

Thanks also to Nigel Lutt of the Bedford Records Office in aiding the research for my trip, and to Robin Holgate of the Luton Museum for his help concerning the history of the 5th Battalion, Bedfordshire & Hertfordshire Regiment. A special mention to my Mum Dot, sister Brenda, Brother-in-law Jim and all the rest of my family and friends for supporting me in my wonderful adventure that was for Dad.

And last but not least, thanks to all the wonderful friends I made on my trip. It would not have been the same without you.

5956247 Pte. COX G C
H.Q.3. 5th Battalion,
Bedfordshire & Hertfordshire Regiment.

DEDICATION

This book is dedicated to the memory of my father and to all those men, women and children who suffered and died at the hands of the Japanese during World War II and since.

A special mention to the men who served with the Bedfordshire & Hertfordshire Regiment in the Far East. My Dad was one of them.

5956247 Pte. COX G C
H.Q.3. 5th Battalion,
Bedfordshire & Hertfordshire Regiment.

My Father and Mother in 1967, shortly before his death.

INTRODUCTION

My father, George Colin Cox, was born at 31 Foster Street, Bedford on 5 March 1915, the youngest of two brothers who would later both become Prisoners of War of the Japanese, his brother to die as a POW on 12th September 1944.

My father always wanted to go back to the Far East to visit his brother's memorial, visit his comrade's graves and, I suppose, lay old ghosts to rest. I remember when I was just 19 years of age, shortly before his death, I found him sitting at the dining room table deep in thought.

"What's up Dad?" I asked him.

"I was just thinking how good it would be to see the Far East again in peacetime," he said.

Sadly, this wish would never materialise for him. He died on 9th July 1968, aged just 53, and I know that his experiences as a POW contributed to his early death (as far back as I can remember my father was never in good health).

I never forgot his wish and I feel very privileged that I have been able to fulfil it for him.

Most of the information concerning my Dad's life out in the Far East I researched myself, as most men who had been

Japanese prisoners of war, including my Dad, never talked much about their experiences as they were too painful.

This book, as well as telling my personal experiences, is about them all. My trip to Singapore and Thailand was for Dad, his brother and for the rest of my family to keep in our hearts the thought that Dad's wish was fulfilled, because we all loved him very much.

FOREWORD

My father, along with the rest of the Beds & Herts and other Regiments of the 18th Division left Liverpool at the end of October 1941 on the Ship *Orcades*. Its intended destination was the Middle East, but as a result of Japan's entry into the War, the Division was diverted to the Far East. The first port of call was to be Halifax, Nova Scotia where the 18th Division boarded a larger ship, the USS *West Point*. This ship was to take them all the way to their destination, Keppel Harbour, Singapore. During the journey, the 18th Division had seen 27 enemy aircraft and had had news from Malaya that things were not going well. It was considered that the *West Point*, along with other ships carrying other Regiments, would be turned round and sent to Batavia, Java's capital, but this was not to be. These men, including my father were now in General Wavell's hands and landed on Singapore Island on 29 January 1942, to be 'thrown in at the deep end' so to speak. The only weapons these men had on landing in Singapore were their rifles and ammunition; there was no air power covering them or to help them in their forthcoming plight. All British planes were fighting in Europe, which was more important at that time to the Government. Tanks were non-existent also. These men stood no chance against the Japanese with their planes, tanks, guns and plenty of ammunition. There were so many unnecessary deaths. The rest is History.

In My Father's Footsteps

The Beginning of it all...

I was staring straight at it, an 'ad' in our local paper. It said 'TRIP TO BURMA' – not that I thought for a moment that I would be going, but oh, how it interested me! I mentioned it to Mum. She was interested and we both thought it would be a good idea to contact the British Legion to find out if they would help financially. Unfortunately, they could not. Meanwhile, Mum, who is getting on a bit now, decided that for her the trip would be a bit too much. So it just left me pondering the whole idea. I racked my brains, working out how much money I would need for the trip and then I suddenly remembered an insurance policy that I had been paying £1.20 into for twenty odd years. Everything seemed to be fitting into place. I sent off my deposit and my name was added to the list of ex-servicemen and relatives from all over the country going on the trip. The excitement was so intense during these first few weeks that I could not sleep. I kept thinking about being able to walk in my Dad's footsteps and doing the one thing he always wanted to do – put flowers at his brother's Memorial at Kranji Cemetery, Singapore.

This whole thing was bringing me much closer to my Dad and I had a strange feeling that he knew. I had to calm down a bit because it was only October and we didn't start our trip until February so I made myself think about Christmas shopping instead, which helped a lot, sleepwise.

ALMOST TIME TO GO

Christmas came and went, and now my trip was all I could think about. As 13th February was getting nearer I was getting cold feet. I would lie in bed thinking to myself, 'What am I doing flying all those thousands of miles, half way around the world with strangers, people I have not even met.' I only had to think about my Dad and my train of thought changed completely. The night before my trip, I even said to my husband that I didn't know if I wanted to go now – and I meant it. Morning came and I was on my way, with George driving, and me sitting in the back of the car with my 9-year-old son. This was something that I just *had* to do.

Heathrow

Other than my suitcases, I had a big bag of goodies for my young son. I had been worried all this time about leaving him for two weeks as I had never left him before. He had had time to get used to the idea and his Dad was having time off work. I knew he would be all right but still felt guilty at leaving him. I had explained to him months ago that it meant a lot to me to be able to go and that I would not have the chance again. He was upset at first but soon got used to the idea, especially when I said I would bring him back, amongst other things a kimono. I was sure this trip was meant to be and something compelled me to go.

We all arrived at the checking in point at Heathrow. There were a few other people there with name badges on like myself, so I knew I was in the right place. I had a few words with one or two of them, which made me feel a little better about leaving my family behind.

GOODBYE

Well this was it. I said my goodbyes, trying not to get too upset. They both looked as choked up as I felt. I was waving to them before turning the corner to board the plane and bang, I had turned left instead of right. As I righted myself they were both smiling at what I had done, and their smiles imprinted themselves on me for the long flight ahead. As soon as I had boarded the plane at 11.00 am, our time, tears came to my eyes. I was missing them already, but made myself think about the wonderful adventure that was ahead of me, and the feeling that I was doing this for my Dad kept me going.

On the plane I sat next to a lady that I would be sharing a room with on the trip. Her name was Rita. We started talking and it made me feel a lot better. I still had no idea who all the other people were. It was a very long flight. We had to fly first to Bangkok – which was about 11 hours and from there on to Singapore, another 3 hours, making a total of 14 hours from Heathrow. I was travelling with Thai International Airways, so there was an oriental feeling from start to finish. Meals on the plane were good and broke the monotony of just sitting for most of the time. I could not sleep either. I was excited and a bit worried about getting to know everyone, whether they would like me and vice versa. As it turned out I need not have worried because they were the best bunch of people I had met in my life and a strong emotional bond was made between us all during the next two weeks.

We arrived at Bangkok and boarded another plane for Singapore. The Thai people greeted us all by bowing their heads with their hands together, saying 'sawadee', which means 'welcome' in Thai. We returned this welcome by doing the same, remembering the old saying. "When in Rome, do as the Romans do". In this case it was, "when in Thailand do as the Thai's do". I was very glad we did not have so long on this flight because my feet had swollen to twice their normal size due to sitting for so long. At last, after another three hours we arrived at Singapore Airport. The time was 12.00am local time (Singapore is 8 hours ahead of Greenwich Mean Time.)

As soon as we got outside, the heat and humidity hit us. I have never known a heat like it. So dry yet so hot. The best way of describing it is like walking into an almost hot oven.

We were told before leaving England by our organiser that we would have to slow down and walk at a pace that was comfortable. I can assure you that we all did. It took almost a week to acclimatise ourselves. I must say, the first thought that entered my head on feeling this heat was 'How on earth did British prisoners of war cope with it, along with near starvation, slave labour, ill-treatment and disease.'

Singapore

Singapore Airport was the cleanest airport I had ever seen. Outside grew the most beautiful orchids, lilies, rhododendrons and flowers of every colour you could think of. Beautiful bushes and trees grew even in this humid, dry climate. Then I remembered my Dad telling me about the monsoons that they have out here, so that accounted for it all.

There was one particular tree that looked like a huge fan. I also thought to myself that during the war out here, none of this would have been at all beautiful to POW's, however many flowers had been planted here.

We were told before landing at Singapore that policing was very strict and not to throw any rubbish or even cigarette ends on the floor, unless you wanted a fine of 200 Singapore dollars (about £150)! Even jaywalking carried a $200fine; pedestrian bridges had to be used when crossing the road.

Eventually our coach arrived to take us all very hot people to our Hotel. We were greeted with a large banner saying 'Welcome Three Pagoda POW Group'. We were greeted with this sign wherever we went. The sign of the Three Pagodas relates to three small ancient temples that are located at the point where the infamous railway built by POWs and forced-labourers crosses the Thai-Burma border. The total length of the railway from Bangkok in Thailand to Thanbyuzayat in Burma is over 400 kilometres.

As we got onto the coach to go to our hotel, we were all given necklaces made from flowers. We were made very welcome. Buttonholes of orchids were also given to us. Our coach was air conditioned, thankfully and we all soon felt a bit cooler.

There were 27 of us on the coach and I really had not had time yet to get to know anyone, except the person I was to be sharing a room with for the next fortnight. I must say at this stage that it was a very welcome piece of information from one of the POW's Arthur Lane, who had served with the Manchester Regiment, that we were to have a 'drinks box' on the coach wherever we went. At least we would not be thirsty on the hectic days of travelling in this heat that was ahead of us.

We all started to introduce ourselves and I found that there were seven former POWs, four widows of POWs, five daughters and two brothers of POWs and various others who had their own reasons for coming on the trip. At last our coach was ready for the off to take us to the Furama Hotel which is situated in the Chinatown District of Singapore, near to places we would be visiting during the next three days. It was also the Chinese New Year and there were lanterns everywhere.

The hotel was very posh, but it was nice just to have a coffee and a rest on the bed because of my swollen feet.

We all had the day to ourselves to do whatever we wanted, so after having a rest and getting ready Rita, my room-mate and I went to look around the shops and to find a telephone to ring home. I was feeling very homesick. I was so far away from home and thought, what on earth am I doing here. As soon as I heard their voices I broke down in tears. They all sounded fine and I felt a lot better.

My son asked, 'Mum have you bought my kimono yet?' That was it, I said 'Right here I go, I am off to get you one now'. I chose a green one with a dragon on the back sewn very beautifully.

Evening came, and Rita and I went down to the Hotel Bar for a drink. Here is where I got to know everyone – one person especially, Linda. She was also here because her Dad, like mine, had been a Japanese POW. He had only died recently. She, like myself, had left her family behind and felt homesick. We got on really well together and cheered each other up tremendously. We both got to know everybody really well over the next few days and I am glad to say we did not get homesick anymore. I still had some emotional calls home during my two weeks away, but they were not due to homesickness, but to some of the sights and emotional moments of my trip.

Battle Sites

We all piled on the coach at about 8.30 am after all having had a good breakfast. Our guide whilst we were in Singapore was to be a gentleman called Bhajan (Budgie for short) and he was indeed a gentleman. As most Singaporeans speak good English, we could understand him perfectly. He also explained everything very well.

As we were travelling through the heart of Singapore we saw some beautiful sights and buildings. The roads, one of which I can remember was Bukit Timor Road. Prisoners of War would remember this road, as a lot of them were made to march by the Japanese the 20 miles or more to the notorious Changi Prison and Changi Village on capitulation.

The roads then would have been dirt tracks but now are proper cemented roadways (tarmac would obviously not withstand the heat out here). In the middle of the roads flowers grew for as far as you could see. Most of the homes and buildings the rich of Singapore occupied were large white houses with carved ebony elephants and suchlike adorning the entrances. Against the white of the houses they looked beautiful. The Lion of Singapore also had its place. Skyscrapers loomed high as we drove onwards.

The poorer people, before, during and after the war lived in what were called Kampongs, which were shacks with back yards where usually a pig and chickens were kept. Now these have been done away with and high rise flats have been built.

The coach stopped. We were now looking onto Singapore from the opposite side of the harbour. We could see the Sultan's Palace, which looked very small from where we were. The Causeway was also in view. This was where Singapore eventually fell, in February 1942, when the Japanese infiltrated the island by coming through the jungle. A lot of our troops, especially the Cambridgeshires, lost their lives defending this Causeway. Molly, who was on the trip with us, could only just remember her father. He died at this stage of the War, perhaps defending the Causeway.

Immediately prior to the outbreak of war, Allied troops numbered 50,000. The number of Japanese troops who were on the front line at the outbreak of war was over 100,000. Due to the lack of knowledge by our Government of the true state of affairs in Singapore, our troops never stood a chance. The Japanese had planes, tanks and plenty of ammunition. Our troops ammunition was running out. It seemed Sir Winston Churchill believed that the Japanese could never take

Fortress Singapore because it was too well defended. On being told the true state of affairs by his Generals, Sir Winston declared that the men were to fight on and "if it came to it all officers should die with their men". When the surrender of Singapore eventually took place on 15th February 1942 there were 130,000 British and Commonwealth troops who became prisoners of war. Many of them died in captivity.

Instead of taking Singapore by sea, the Japanese came in through the jungle. They were used to the heat and the jungle as Japan's climate is very similar. Our troops had not even been properly trained in jungle warfare. By this time the Japanese were all over Malaya and Allied troops were having to retreat.

About half a mile to the right of us we could see the Naval Base, which my Dad, along with the rest of the Beds & Herts Regiment were defending. It was hard to imagine my Dad having been here in this hot place that seemed to be a different world from the one I knew. It felt as if I was seeing things all over again for him through my eyes. He would have been very touched to think I was out here experiencing his past, the past he would have liked to experience for himself. I felt honoured to be able to do this for him – but the more emotional historical sights were yet to come…

After the fall of Singapore in February 1942 it was revealed that Allied losses on the Island itself were around 7,000 killed and 2,000 missing. The total number of deaths by the end of the War in Singapore and Thailand including British, Australian, American and Dutch Servicemen was in excess of 150,000. Of these 100,000 were forced labourers from Burma, Malaya, India, Indonesia and China. They were treated abominably by the Japanese.

We were once again on the coach, travelling this time to visit what was once the Ford factory. The Japanese shot many nurses, who had been tending the wounded, here behind the factory, but before doing so, had their 'bit of fun' by raping them first.

The next historical site was a Memorial which stood on a mass grave site dedicated to thousands of men, women and children who were killed or murdered by the Japanese. Japanese soldiers who had died during the fighting for Singapore were buried here also, which seemed rather ironic, taking into consideration that they killed women and children as well as our own men and lay alongside them.

This Memorial was situated on the outskirts of Singapore and had been known to POW's as River Valley Camp. There were over a hundred stone steps leading up to it. For the making of this mass grave the Japanese forced our troops, many of them from the different Regiments which comprised the 18th Division, to scrape and dig dirt from a huge hill, carrying it as best they could to where the mass grave was situated. This took some time as the POWs had no proper tools and had to dig and scrape with anything they could find. After all the dead bodies had been dragged to the top of the hill to be buried or cremated, the dirt was put on top. This feat killed a lot of the men who were already exhausted and injured, but the rest had to carry on until it was finished. By this time a lot of the bodies were decomposing because of the intense heat and together with the stench and the flies the job must have been unbearable. Beatings and killings were commonplace. If you could not work, you were no good to the Japanese. But worse was yet to come for these men.

Our next stop was the Alexandra Hospital. A horrendous massacre took place here. The Japanese decided that our badly injured troops would not be of any use to them, so the easiest way to solve the problem was to kill them. Their bayonets spared no-one. Doctors and nurses were also killed and anyone else who got in the way. A memorial stands here in honour of all who died. It was very hard to take in all the terrible things that happened. It is a wonder that anyone survived at all. By what our POW friends told us it was just sheer luck if you made it home. We were all getting quite close to each other by this time, and were sharing a great deal of emotion.

FORT CANNING

I had not before my trip heard of Fort Canning and I do not suppose many ordinary soldiers had seen it either during the War. We were lucky because the Secret Underground Bunkers had only just been opened up to the public, and we were to be some of the first to see them. Fort Canning during the war had been Army H.Q. The troops fate was decided here and the surrender to the Japanese Imperial Army.

As we walked into Fort Canning there were high green grassed mounds with a large iron gate in the middle of them. It felt a bit eerie on entering. There was a dank musty smell and a feeling of dampness, which was not surprising, after all it had been closed up for nearly 50 years. It was exactly the same inside as it had been left all those years ago. There were old fashioned tables and chairs piled away in one room. Another room still had the holes in the walls where the switchboard and radio transmitters had been ripped away. Writing in Japanese was still on the walls, where they had tried to decipher messages. It was like a maze inside. Passages leading in all different directions for I suppose taking secret messages or for a quick escape. I found it very claustrophobic and was glad to get outside once again, even though the heat was unbearable. It had felt as if we had gone back in time and it gave you a weird feeling.

I hoped that the photographs I had taken inside would come out all right, which reminded me to buy some more film. I had already used up two films and it was only Day 3. All in all on my trip I used 12 films, most with 36 exposures.

KRANJI WAR CEMETERY

This, I knew was going to be the most emotional part of the trip so far for me. The coach drew up alongside a sign saying Kranji War Cemetery. Whilst I was here I had to find out from the War Graves Record Books whether a Percy Maddams was interred here at Kranji (my brother-in-law's uncle). He had died as a POW early on during the war, but his name unfortunately was not listed. Perhaps I would have better luck at Kanchanaburi. I had a great feeling of excitement inside me. To think that after all these years I would be able to take all this home on film to show my Mum and the rest of my family. It was unbelievable, even to think I was here. Linda, my new friend was also going to film me at my Uncle's Memorial with her video camera. It was all so wonderful. If there is anything up there I thought, my head raised towards the sky, my Dad's got to be with me now.

I bought some lovely purple flowers for the uncle I had never known and started to walk through the open gates. It was so beautiful and peaceful here. On entering the gates the first thing I saw was a white memorial stone about 12 x 6 feet which said "THEIR NAMES LIVETH FOR EVERMORE". There were hundreds of gravestones, all of them white and I walked around and looked at quite a lot of them, those of men from different Regiments and of different races that were our Allies. Those which struck at my heart most were inscribed 'A Soldier known only unto God'. I did not know any of these men but the emotion overpowered all of us and I had not even got as far as my Uncle's Memorial yet. I left the gravestones and started walking up the steep incline which led to the Huge Memorial. In front of the Memorial walls stood a large bevelled Stone about 40' x 20' beautifully worded. It read:

ON THE WALLS OF THIS MEMORIAL ARE RECORDED THE NAMES OF 24,000 SOLDIERS AND AIRMAN OF MANY RACES UNITED IN SERVICE TO THE BRITISH CROWN WHO GAVE THEIR LIVES IN MALAYA AND NEIGHBOURING LANDS AND SEAS AND IN THE AIR OVER SOUTHERN AND EASTERN ASIA BUT TO WHOM THE FORTUNES OF WAR DENIED THE CUSTOMARY RIGHTS ACCORDED TO THEIR COMRADES IN DEATH. THEY DIED FOR ALL FREE MEN.

Now I was looking at the Memorial. It must have been at least 200 yards long and thirty to forty feet high and was shaped as if it was a ship or boat, with wall after wall of 24,000 soldiers, sailors and airmen's names running along the entire length of them. There was a huge shape like the funnel of a ship on top of the Memorial that reached to the sky which must have signified 'land, sea and air'. The most had certainly been done for these men in death if not in life.

Now, at last, to find my Uncle. I was looking for Column 16. The Regiment of Royal Artillery 2nd Heavy Ack Ack, Gunner 1603286 Richard Charles Cox. Linda was with me and my heart started pounding, and there it was R C COX, staring straight at me. Just seeing the name made me cry. My emotions were in a turmoil. I was thinking of my Dad, my Uncle, my Mum, wishing my Dad was there with me, thinking that I was the very first, and probably the last one of my family to ever come out here. After 50 years to be able to do this for my Dad and to pay all our respects to my uncle who never came home was almost unbelievable. For the first time in years I was speechless.

Linda suddenly broke my silence by saying she wanted to get me on film. So I laid flowers for my uncle, the first he had ever had since his death – and was telling Linda on film about how my uncle had been out here in Singapore and Thailand as a POW and how he had also been with my Dad in prison camps along the railway some of the time. He died aged 31 on the 12 September 1944 on the Japanese Transport ship, *Rakuyo Maru*, which was taking POWs to Japan to work in the mines. This ship was sunk by USS *Sealion* because the Japanese refused to fly Red Cross flags. Unfortunately, this happened to many transport ships carrying prisoners of war.

My Uncle Richard, known as Dick, left a wife Ruby, whom he had only married the day before he set sail for the Far East. She died about three years ago and never re-married. They had been childhood sweethearts and she never got over his death. He had been the only one for her. As far as I know she never made it out here.

Molly, another daughter, found her father's name on the Kranji Memorial, A B J White. He had served with the Cambridgeshire Regiment. Alan and Dick Fielding had an elder brother whose name was also inscribed here. William Fielding who had served for some time with the Loyal Regiment.

We paid our last respects and on the way back to the coach came across ex-POW Jimmy MacKay, who had unfortunately found a name of a friend he thought had got home. He obviously was quite upset. It seemed on this trip that we were crying in the day and laughing at night, when we had time to relax. It had been a very emotional afternoon for us all. Now we were all ready for a long cold drink and a rest on the coach. I tried to have a little shut-eye on the coach, but my mind would not let me. It was full of too many thoughts.

That evening after a well earned rest, we all had a date at a Cantonese Restaurant called the Four Seasons. This is where Jimmy MacKay took off his POW Days and did his loin cloth act using a serviette. It was good to think he could still have a little joke about it. I think most of the POWs learnt to enjoy life even more after what they went through. It did not seem to take a lot to please them. They were all smashing people.

Getting back to the Restaurant, it was all very posh and the service was first class. There were turntables so that you could easily get a bit of everything. You just turned the table round to what ever it was you were after, but I could not eat hardly any of it. There were things to eat that I had never seen before, squid, different sorts of seafood and fish of every type just laying on the table as if they had come straight out of the river, eyes the lot. I am afraid this was not for me, but I had a laugh watching everyone else tucking in. I suppose I should have made myself eat some of it as I know the POWs during their captivity would have given anything for the smallest morsel, and no doubt so would I.

A joke did come out of it all though. As I am rather a portly person ex-POW Jim Smith, another Jim, who had served with the Loyal & North Lancashire Regiment said to me, "You ought to come and live out here, you would soon lose some weight!" My answer to that was "You are not so thin yourself, you old codger!" and he wasn't. I am afraid "old codger" has stuck with him now. When he calls me on the phone he always says in his broad Lancashire accent "Is Part Thar" and I say "Hello you old codger", which carries on into "Many a tune played on an old fiddle, etc, etc." But although he was only joking, he was right. Other than not liking the food very much, I did not get that hungry, I suppose because of the heat, but I did make sure I had lots to drink.

Linda noticed that I was not eating very much so she gave me a good tip, to make a couple of rolls up at breakfast and put them in the fridge in my room for later. This I did every morning by wrapping them in a serviette and hiding them in my handbag. At least now I would not starve.

As it happened, I lost a stone during the first few days of being here, probably due to all the sweating I did as well. They all used to laugh at me, because every time I got on the coach after one of our visits, my tops were always saturated around the neck and were so wet that they looked a different colour from the bottom part. I have always found it hard to handle the heat and it was not because I was a big girl either, some of them were fatter than me, well one or two of them anyway, and they were not perspiring at all. Although it is supposed to be good to let it all out rather than keeping it in, it is very uncomfortable. The only times I felt cool, were on the coach or at the Hotel.

As soon as we arrived back from the Restaurant to the Hotel, the first thing I had to do was to ring home to make sure everyone, especially my little boy, was all right. He seemed to be coping quite well with me away and always seemed cheerful on the phone. I missed him a lot, and the cuddles, but before I went to bed I had to let them know all the latest news and I went to sleep that night thinking what an emotional but wonderful day it had been.

Changi

Woke up this morning with mosquito bites all over my legs. I had been using insect repellent but it could not have done much good. Today we were going to Changi and Roberts Barracks, which was to turn out to be as emotional, if not more so, than my visit to Kranji Cemetery. The reason being that from now on I would be walking in my father's footsteps.

CHANGI

As the coach approached Changi I had a view of the high stone grey walls of the notorious Changi Gaol. I could see the solemn armed sentries in their towers which stood at each corner of the Gaol. It was a terrible looking place and sent a shiver through me. It was still being used as a maximum security prison.

The coach stopped alongside a small wooden Chapel. This was a replica of the original built by the Australian POWs during their captivity and was now dedicated to the men that had died. The original had been shipped to Australia as it was mainly Australian troops that were actually imprisoned inside Changi Gaol on capitulation.

My father along with the rest of the Beds & Herts Regiment and men from other Regiments were fenced in around the outside of Changi Gaol, which one of my Dad's old pals told me they called 'The Pit'. Some men from other Regiments were imprisoned nearby at Selerang and Roberts Barracks, which we were to visit later that morning. My father along with a lot of other men from his Regiment were imprisoned inside Changi Gaol after work on the Railway had been completed. The Chapel was a crude open air building made from wood, an exact replica of the original with a garden surrounding it full of tropical bushes, trees and flowers. The Altar had a Gold Cross upon it which I found out had been made by some of the POWs out of old bullet shells. There were some wreaths made from silk flowers adorning the Altar and anyone wanting to, could pick a flower from the garden and lay it upon the Altar.

Similar to our churches in England, there were rows of benches to sit on facing the Chapel for when a Service was held.

From the Chapel we could all see the Changi Prison clock tower looming high above us and there was not one of us surveying this that did not give a thought to all those men who did not get home.

The next port of call was the Changi Museum which was only a few yards away from the Chapel.

The Museum was only a shack type affair. Inside were Regimental Badges of the different Regiments that had served and been held captive here during the war. On show were old tools that had been found since the war which had been used by the men working on the railway.

There were enlarged prints that had been taken from old photographs of men who were almost skeletons. They had been taken at different Prison camps. I had seen similar photographs, but not as terrible as the ones here. It saddened me to look at them and I wondered how many men had actually made it home and got through their 3½ years of hell. Most of these photographs had been taken on Liberation, but the odd one or two had been taken as evidence of brutality by Prisoners in the hope that if Liberation did not come, justice would be done. Any prisoner who was found to have in his possession photographs, maps, writing of any sort or a radio was killed, usually by beheading, which would always be a public spectacle. There were also photographs of Japanese Officers – at this point I wondered if they were human at all.

From what I had learnt I knew how cruelly the Japanese had treated POWs. To the Japanese, to be a prisoner was worse than death and to die for the Emperor – who to them was a god – was the highest honour that could be bestowed upon them. So to the Japanese these POWs lacked honour and were looked upon as cowards. That is one of the reasons POWs were treated so badly. When Japan surrendered in August 1945 many Japanese committed Hara-Kiri, some because of the terrible atrocities they had gladly taken part in, and knew the hangman's noose would be awaiting them.

On our way out of the Museum most of us wrote in the Changi Memorial Book. I wrote:

"I am here for my Dad who was once at Changi and whom I loved very much."

Linda and I decided we would like to get a closer look at Changi Prison and take a few photographs. Both our Dads had been here and it was only 100 yards away from the Museum. There was a road alongside the Prison and we walked up the stone steps to cross the road. We both wanted to stand in front of the Prison Gates – the gates our Dads would have walked through. The sentries were looking at us, but we had come a long way from home to do this, whether we were supposed to or not; we had to do it. We both stood there with tears running down our cheeks, hoping that our Dads knew we were here, each of us knowing that we were walking in our father's footsteps. We just managed through our tears to take a photograph of each other. These emotional moments would be with us for the rest of our lives.

We met up with the others who had decided to have a walk around Changi Village. Firstly we had to find a toilet, which turned out to be a hole in the floor, where, I found out later, I had been bitten by some insect, probably a mosquito.

Molly and I decided we needed to buy hats to protect us from the sun, so we had a walk to the shops. We bought ourselves wide-brimmed straw hats that would protect our shoulders as well.

Nothing much had changed it seemed in this village since the war. There were no new buildings except for some flats that we saw on our way back to the coach.

It was now our last visit of the day. We were heading for Roberts Barracks where mainly Australians were taken on capitulation. As we were driving through the gates ex-POW Arthur Lane pointed out a large building which he said the Japanese had occupied. There were palm trees and different sorts of bushes growing at each side of the building with smaller shrubs and flowers at the front. It was hard to believe that this place was once infected by the Japanese Imperial Army – with all our troops at their mercy.

We got off the coach near to the Barracks and were told by our guide, 'Budgie', that we were going to see what had once been the Dysentery Ward, but was now used as a Chapel in honour of Prisoners of War. It was not very big inside, but I expect it had been full of sick men, may be even my Dad. I stood in front of the Altar and had my photograph taken. It was then that I saw the famous murals. One was of Jesus on the Cross which said 'Father Forgive Them They Know Not What They Do'. These Murals had been painted on the walls by a POW whilst in the Dysentery Ward. He used materials such as grass, leaves and flowers which other prisoners brought him when they could. He even used his own blood. These Murals were painted over but kept reappearing. Nothing would cover them for long. Some people seem to think it was because of natural materials used; others thought it may be an Act of God. Whatever the answer, it was all very moving.

Once again, we were on the coach heading for the Hotel. We had another free afternoon, so after a drink and a rest I decided to get some film developed to make sure my new camera was working all right. Rita, my room-mate came with me and we then decided to have a look around the shops.

I purchased some lovely little jewelled elephants to give as presents. We were both getting a bit hungry by now, so the best place to go was 'McDonalds' which we enjoyed much more than Cantonese.

Tomorrow we would be leaving Singapore and would be flying to Bangkok – Thailand.

Bangkok

We all left the Furama Hotel – Singapore at 10.30 a.m. to arrive at Bangkok at 2.00 p.m. Bangkok Airport or even Bangkok itself definitely did not come up to the standards of Singapore, but we were made just as welcome.

Once again we were greeted with the Three Pagodas Banner, necklaces of flowers and our new Thai guide called Ron. The coach journey was only supposed to be a short one – taking us to our Hotel which was called the Ambassador. But our ten minute journey took over an hour. None of us could believe the amount of traffic we saw, and were told by Ron our Thai guide that at rush hour a 10 minute drive could sometimes take 2 hours. I have never seen such pandemonium. There were about 5 lanes of traffic on each side of the road. We were told by Ron, that the best form of transport here were scooters or mopeds, as they could zig-zag in and out of the traffic. We did not see one person wearing a helmet and some even had passengers holding young children and babies in their arms. Policemen were stationed at cross roads and junctions directing the traffic wearing dust masks. As we were slowly driving along, you could see the shacks, you could not call them houses, more like hovels, that these people lived in. Some were made from corrugated iron, others from wood. You could see one Thai woman outside her shack throwing water over herself from an old tin bath, completely dressed, and we were told by Ron, that the women washed in this way, with all their clothes on. Something to do with their Religion or Culture. Washing was hanging out to dry everywhere you looked. It seemed to me that there were either rich or poor (mostly poor) in Bangkok and nothing in between. Jim Hill, who was the eldest POW in our party (79 years) and who had served with the Argyle Regiment told us that nothing much had changed with regard to living conditions here since the war.

Ron, was to be our guide from now until the end of our trip. He only looked about 20 years old but was actually 32. They do say that the Thai people look quite young until they reach middle age, they then get old very quickly, probably due to the heat and lots of hard work. They all seemed to smile all the time. I can remember my Dad telling me that, but he called them Siamese, which they were then. That was before Siam came to be known as Thailand.

Ron, was to turn out to be a great entertainer, as well as a good guide, on the sometimes quite long coach trips we had in store for us. The time certainly passed quickly when he was joking around and we all got quite fond of him.

Since our hectic three days in Singapore, whilst in Bangkok we were all going to go sight seeing. More hectic emotional days were ahead of us when we were to be going further North into Thailand.

Work on the infamous Burma-Siam Railway started at Bangkok and groups of men including my Dad were taken (in his case) from Changi in Singapore and loaded into cattle wagons, 30-40 to a truck and transported the 1,200 miles to Bangkok. The heat inside the hot metal wagons must have been unbearable, along with not having much food or water to drink and if the call of nature came (due to dysentery), they were sometimes allowed to relieve themselves by sticking their backsides out of the wagon, with a couple of mates holding on to them. It all depended on whether they were lucky enough to have a more lenient guard. A lot of these men died before they even arrived in Thailand due to lack of food, water and disease.

Once these wagons arrived at their destinations, the men were marched to base camps at Non Pladuc and Bam Pong to start work on the infamous Railway. If the men were not marching fast enough they were beaten with bamboo poles, rifle butts or kicked and slapped about.

If a man could not go on and fell, he was either shot or just left behind. The POWs did all they could for each other, the stronger helping the weaker.

At this camp, as indeed at all camps along the railway, the men had to build themselves what were called Attap Huts. These were made from bamboo and attap leaves. First the men had to build the Japanese officers living quarters before starting their own. Deep trenches also had to be dug which were to be used as latrines with slats of bamboo across them to squat upon. After a while, what with the heat and flies, the stench became unbearable and obviously these living conditions did not help the health of these already deteriorating men. Diseases such as Cholera, Typhus, Beri-Beri and Malaria were commonplace, and when the Monsoons came these trenches along with the huts would become flooded and swept away, leaving a quagmire of mud and excrement. This happened in most of the camps during the monsoon season and that was when Cholera became rife.

The men were getting weaker and weaker but unknown to them at the time they were to be slaves of the Japanese for 3½ years. Perhaps it was just as well they did not know. There was no proper food or medicine. Red Cross parcels had been sent to the men, but the Japanese kept them for themselves. Sometimes drugs were obtained by some brave POW by either stealing them or bartering something of value with a

Japanese guard, such as a watch or cigarette lighter – sometimes the men were able to hide such items, but on being found out, the penalty was death. Such articles had to be hidden very carefully.

We did drive near to where these Base Camps had been, but now the area has been built up with shacks and shanties plus a few shops.

At last, after over an hour in the coach of stopping and starting we were nearing our Hotel. It looked as posh, if not more so, than the Furama at Singapore. As soon as we walked in you could not help noticing the huge Crystal chandeliers. It was a very large hotel and was beautifully furnished. There were also large tropical fish tanks in every part of the foyer. It all looked very oriental. It was absolute heaven to just sit down, and we were all given a welcome drink. After that Rita and I went straight up to our rooms to have a little rest before our River Cruise and Seafood meal that evening on the Chopraya river.

From now until 23 February BBC Scotland were covering our trip on behalf of the Scottish veterans, and were to be including us all on film. It was to be shown on BBC Scotland's News programme. We were also very pleased to learn that film taken of us was going to be put on videotape and sent to everyone as a souvenir.

As well as the BBC being with us, Phillip Sherwell from the *Daily Telegraph* would be joining us at Kanchanaburi, to write an article for his paper about our emotional visits to the cemeteries and Prison camps along the railway.

The time was now 7.00 p.m. and we were all about to board the River Barge that was to take us for our Cruise on the Chopraya River.

Before doing so, some of us decided to change some Travellers cheques as we would be needing a few bahts the next day. There were 36 bahts to the pound.

The Barge was quite large, with brightly-coloured fairy lights adorning it, very picturesque. We were all seated, six to a table and wondered what was in store for us tonight. I know what I would have chosen, given the chance, rump streak, chips, peas and mushrooms. It was not to be. The first course was fish Thai style, what sort of fish I did not know. It still had it's eyes in it's sockets. I made myself nibble as much as possible. Then came the awful seafood platter, and at this point I must say that I wished I had nibbled more of the first course. Some of the others enjoyed it, especially Linda, who had mine as well. There were crabs, oysters and shrimps, you name it, it was there. All with their shells on.

About this time the BBC crew were filming, and they, Alan and Alistair were having great fun watching everyone trying to eat this stuff.

Ahead of me at the front of the Barge was a young Thai girl sitting cross-legged in a very pretty Thai silk dress playing Thai music on a Zither. It felt as if I was in another world. Across the river you could see some of the temples brightly lit up. It was a fantastic sight and I wondered if my Dad would have seen them when he had been here during the war. I know that these temples are very old.

Ron, our guide, told us that every male in Thailand has to devote some part of his life to become a monk, even if it is only for a year. 'That is the Thai way' he said. Whenever Ron was telling us about his culture, he would always use that expression sounding like 'Dat dis de way'.

At last dessert – fruit Thai-style. All types: kiwi fruit, red melon, white melon and little round red fruits. Well, that went down okay. There was one good thing that came out of me not eating much, and that was – I was almost the only one who did not suffer with my stomach.

After our peaceful cruise along the river, the coach then headed back to the Hotel. It was still quite early, so a few of us decided to look at the market stalls just around the corner from our Hotel. It was very crowded, and we were told to keep together and to watch out for our purses and wallets, as Bangkok is not the safest of places. There was not one of us who would have walked around on our own.

Tony, our organiser, told us that it was okay to barter for goods. The price was always knocked down for you, and that was what I did.

I tried bartering for two T-shirt and shorts sets for my nieces, but the stallholder did not seem to want to go as low as I did. I started walking away but he called me back and luckily I got my bargain. This salesman was not very happy for long though, because the rest of my friends tried the same, but he was not having any of it. He shooed them all away and in his own words told them not to come back. It must have been my lucky day.

After our very interesting market trading, we all went to a small cafe to have a drink. It had been another tiring day so we all decided to have a comparatively early night and a nice cool shower to refresh us for our tour of Bangkok tomorrow. Before I went to bed I wanted to ring home to make sure everything was all right – they were and the house had not burnt down yet either. I also wanted to find out if my Mum was all right as she had not been too well – she was fine. I did not realise how much I would miss them and it felt good to hear their voices.

Thailand

This was our last day in Bangkok as tomorrow we would be heading north. Our day was going to be a sightseeing one, visiting amongst other things the Bangkok Temples and Grand Palace. We were told to wear something that covered our shoulders as a sign of respect when entering the temples and to take off our shoes.

It was very hot and humid here and the temperature had reached 35 degrees centigrade. Thank goodness for air conditioning. It was not too bad in the coach but when you stepped outside the heat and humidity hit you. All Hotels are obviously air conditioned and you feel very cool when inside.

Before visiting the Temples we were going to visit a local Gem Shop. The jewellery is actually hand made on the premises. Diamonds and other precious stones of all descriptions are cut and polished on site. The jewellery was still expensive but cheaper to buy here in Thailand compared to some other countries. First we were to see a film showing how these items of jewellery were made.

As we approached the Gem Shop we saw a very solemn Guard standing outside holding a rifle against his shoulder. I felt very uneasy just walking by him. There were parrots, minah birds and monkeys in cages outside, I suppose to attract peoples attention to the shop.

The film was very interesting and showed us the people at work in the small factory that adjoined the shop. We then walked through this factory watching with interest each part of the process from start to finish.

From there we walked straight into the actual jewellery shop. Every item of jewellery you could think of was on display, every stone, colour and size. Unfortunately, the prices were still far too high for me, but a few of our party bought something.

We were once again on the coach heading for the Grand Palace. The amount of traffic on the roads of Bangkok was horrendous. There were no bypasses or Underground system of travel to relieve the congestion and the Highway Code had never been in existence here. No car insurance or tax – it was just a case of looking after number one. All any of us could hear was bib-bib-bib during the whole journey.

As a matter of interest, Ron our guide told us that to buy a new car out here would cost almost twice as much as in England. I suppose that was why there were so many old bangers and trucks to be seen on the roads.

The coach pulled up and we all headed for the Grand Palace, being stopped on the way by young Thai people selling silk painted pictures. I bartered yet again for one of those and thought I had got a bargain until one of our party told me that he had two for almost the same price as my one. Oh well, you cannot win 'em all!

We approached the entrance to the Grand Palace, which was through a door in the wall which surrounded the Temples. They all looked very exotic with gold, jewels and stones shining so brightly in the sunlight. We went from one to the other, taking our shoes on and off, as we went in and out. Ron told us that every stone was put on separately. It must have taken years. At some entrances to the temples there were elephants, dragons and other oriental creatures bejewelled and shining just as brightly. Monks in orange sarongs wandered about, which added a mystical air. We were told that due to their Religion, they were not allowed to touch or be touched, or to get into conversation with a female. It was also an insult to touch any Thai person on the head as it was a sacred part of the body and not to cross your legs in a way you could point a foot at them. So we all tried as best we could to remember not to cross our legs.

Surrounding the Emperor's Palace were very well kept Bonsai trees and bushes. The Monks must be kept very busy around here. Another piece of information that was given to us was that the Thai people contribute as much of their income as they can afford to the Monks. They have to do this, and that is probably why there are quite a few of them. It is mostly farming out here for the Thai people and very hard work for very little. The heat was getting even more unbearable, which again made me reflect upon all those men who were forced to work in it. At least we could have a drink when we liked.

It felt good, once again, to get back on the coach out of the heat. Next on the Agenda was a visit to a Thai Cultural Show. But first, we were to have lunch at the Rose Gardens nearby.

We all piled yet again off the coach, and at once the smell of roses filled your nostrils. It was the first time on this trip something reminded us of home. As soon as we entered the Restaurant we could see two large tables set up with all different sorts of meat (real meat) salad and even chips. This was more like it, with cakes and fruit for afters. We all helped ourselves to as much as we liked, well I certainly did and could not remember being so full since arriving in the Far East.

We were all now walking the short distance to the Thai Cultural Show's 2.45 Performance. There were a lot of people queuing up so we all joined them.

The Show was to be performed in a very large open air type building, similar to the huts that the POW's had to live in. There was a roof made out of straw and leaves with large bamboo poles holding it all together. Even though it was open air, except for having a roof, it was very hot inside, but once everybody found a seat and the show started, the fans were switched on, which made us all feel a lot cooler.

The First Act was Finger Dancing. There were about 100 Thai girls in bright orange jewelled costumes with Oriental headresses on. It was a very exotic sight. The dancing was superb and the way their fingers and wrists moved all meant something to them. The girls learn when very young and have to keep practising for their fingers to keep the curved position. Our guide Ron, told us jokingly that ' they have to hit their fingers with a hammer' and it sure looked that way.

Next came ancient fighting and kickboxing, which was very entertaining. Then came the Bamboo dancing. I can remember my Dad talking to me about this type of dancing, so he must have seen it done somewhere. It was done very well and must have been quite dangerous. The Bamboo Poles were very thick and were held by one person at each end. They would be clicked together, opening and closing whilst the girls danced back and forth, the pace being quickened up as the girls were dancing. One step wrong and an ankle could be broken. 'Rather them than me', I thought.

The show lasted about an hour, after which we all needed a drink. We saw a man selling drinks at a much smaller hut.

Nearby, were a group of elephants picking up logs, generally showing off I think and on each elephants back sat a Mahout.

I was, surprisingly, given my drink in a hollowed out bamboo cup, which gave flavour to the whole setting. The man selling the drinks could see that I was taken by this cup, and said I could keep it, which pleased me very much. What with looking at the elephants and my bamboo cup my thoughts, yet again, were going back to things my Dad had told me about years ago, when I had been quite small, about how the elephants would help the prisoners by pushing and pulling up trees. He had also told me that sometimes an elephant would refuse to carry a log or tree that was too heavy. That was when the Japanese guards would make the men carry it on their shoulders, more often than not wounding themselves as the bamboo cut into their shoulders or fell on their feet. Once bamboo broke the skin, tropical ulcers would develop, which ate into the flesh right down to the bone. Because of lack of medication due to the Japanese refusing to hand over Red Cross parcels, these ulcers became infected so badly that they would have to be scraped out by the Medics with instruments such as the sharpened edge of a spoon, often without any sort of anaesthetic. Many men had to have limbs amputated due to gangrene setting in but a large number of prisoners died nonetheless. The Medics did the very best they could with what they had and saved a great many lives.

Without these Medics there would have been no tomorrow for any of these men.

Jim Smith and Arthur Lane, two of the ex-POW's I have mentioned previously, told me that a lot of the chaps, including themselves, would put maggots into the wounds to eat away the dead flesh and pus, but they soon felt it when the maggots started to eat the good flesh. That was the time to remove them. I can remember asking my Dad about the deep round scar on his leg, I expect they all had them. It was a miracle any POWs' survived the ill-treatment and disease that was inflicted upon them.

Linda suddenly nudged me back to the present, to tell me that I would be left behind if I did not hurry up.

This evening we were going to a Thai Reunion Dinner at the Pitman Restaurant where a Colonel Longman from the British Embassy was to greet us all, especially the POWs. Maybe there would be time to have a little rest before then.

Rita, my roommate decided to give it a miss. She was a lot older than I was and felt totally worn out. The heat certainly took it out of you. I did not mind her not going in the least, but I definitely was not going to miss out on anything.

The Pitman Restaurant was not very far and we all got off the coach dressed to the nines. The men looked very smart with their little dickey bows and all us ladies looked as radiant as we could in our posh dresses. We were all greeted once again by some exotically dressed Thai girls holding our banner, with another putting flowered necklaces over our heads. We had to go up a flight of stairs to the Restaurant. It was all very elegant with four tables about 40 feet long running from one end of the room to the other. The tables were very low and we all realised that we were going to have to eat sitting on the floor Thai style.

There was a drop underneath the very low tables where your legs would have to dangle. If you were lucky and had quite long legs you could reach the bottom, but Daisy, whose husband had died as a POW in Japan, could not reach the bottom and had to keep wriggling to stay put. At 83 she did well to sit like that, even us younger ones were getting a bit of backache. Pat Heap, another lady with us, whose husband had died as a prisoner at Chungkai had to have a chair and ate from a tray on her lap. I almost followed suit, but if Daisy could do it, then so could I. We all sat, or should I say fell down, whilst the waiters and waitresses served us. There was a stage straight in front of us all from where Thai dancing girls suddenly appeared. These again were very exotically dressed and danced expertly and elegantly, similar to the dancers at the Cultural Show that afternoon.

The Thai meal was not too bad considering I did not like the stuff very much, but there was a lot more to choose from, so I did not do too badly. Linda did even better and finished mine off as well. The dancing continued with an Ancient Thai Lovers Quarrel which was done very artistically. The BBC cameras were very busy and we were all clicking away with ours. Most of us had already used three or four films and would be using a lot more in the days to come.

When the dancing finished the POWs were called up onto the stage for a group photo, holding the banner in front of them. Everyone was cheering and there was not one of us that did not feel pleased for these men, that they had survived all that they had been through and were standing here tonight, even if it had taken them 50 years to be able to do so – to lay old ghosts to rest and to visit their comrade's graves.

We were all then ushered up onto the stage with them for another photograph along with Colonel Longman from the British Embassy. The evening had been grand and our visit to Bangkok an experience. Tomorrow we would be leaving for the Kwai Region where our historical emotional journey to visit the cemeteries and POW Camp sites along the railway would begin. I would definitely be walking in my Dad's footsteps from now on.

River Kwai and Kanchanaburi

The coach was once again on its way and getting well into the countryside. Although Bangkok had been an experience, the places we would now be visiting was the main reason we were all here. Our feelings were mixed. I for one, felt excitement, sadness and happiness all rolled into one at the thought of all the sights I was going to see. It meant so much to me the fact that I would be covering ground that my father had walked on and I would be able to grasp a part of his life that he never really talked about. It was an honour to be able to do this for him and I knew that all my family at home were following my movements from day to day via a copy of the Itinerary I had left them. It would have been wonderful to have shared this trip with my Dad, but may be I was, I often had that feeling.

The POW's who were with us would have a lot to cope with emotionally. Seeing again all these places where they were once held captive, under such terrible circumstances and visiting their comrades graves for the first time. We all felt very deeply for them.

Our first stop was going to be Kanchanaburi Cemetery. POWs who had been here during their captivity had called it Kanburi for short. The Cemeteries out here are situated near to where the actual Prison camps had been and are under the keeping of the Commonwealth War Graves Commission. The remains of the men who had died as POWs were moved after the war from their crude grave sites and interred in Cemeteries such as Kanchanaburi. The Kanburi Prison camp had been a large one and a great many men had died here.

The first thing I had to do at this cemetery was to find out whether my brother-in-law's uncle had been interred here. Like my father, he had served with the 5th Battalion of the Beds & Herts Regiment. My brother-in-law had known he had died as a POW but never knew where, when or even if he had a grave. I bought some flowers in the hope of finding him, if not I would leave them for one of the other unfortunate men. It was a very strange feeling for me to think that my feet may tread in exactly the same place as my father's. He may have even known this man I was looking for.

We could all now see as the coach stopped the entire cemetery. Row after row of small grey stones raised slightly from their bed in the ground. Hundreds of young men who had died so unnecessarily. Most of the men would have been in their teens and twenties, some in their thirties and some would have been my Dad's mates. The Japanese had no excuses for the sights we were seeing now. It tore at your heart to think of what all these poor men had gone through before their death. It was their own mates who had to either bury them or cremate them in all the camps.

We were now approaching the entrance to the cemetery which read Kanchanaburi War Cemetery 1939-45. It was made from white stone with a little roof and three archways which you could walk through. On entering one could see a Memorial on the wall which was black with gold lettering and read:

'In Honoured Remembrance of the fortitude and Sacrifice of the valiant company who perished while building the Railway from Thailand to Burma during their long captivity.
Those who have no known grave are commemorated by name at Rangoon Singapore and Hong Kong and their comrades rest in the three war cemeteries of Kanchanaburi, Chungkai and Thanbyuzayat

"I will make you a name and a praise among all people of the earth when I turn back your captivity before your eyes saith the Lord."

Underneath this Memorial was a stone ledge and resting on this ledge was the Memorial Register which we all signed in turn. Tears were being shed by all.

A high hedge surrounded the cemetery with a very large Memorial Cross sitting in the middle towards the end. Trees, bushes, shrubs and flowers grew in abundance of every colour. All the gravestones were the same, equally spaced out with a walkway in between each line. The stones were about 15 x 15 inches and 6 inches high, coloured grey. Hundreds and hundreds of them.

The heat was almost unbearable. Cut flowers do not last long out here in this sort of climate, but it would be wonderful if I could find the name I was looking for. Arthur Lane who was asking for the War Graves Record Books had been a Prisoner here himself. In fact most of our party of POWs had. They all had someone to find. It came to my turn for Arthur to look up the name I wanted and to my surprise there he was.

PERCY R MADDAMS, who had died aged 24 on 25 August 1943. I had found it, my brother-in-laws uncle, who like my uncle, had not had anyone visit his grave in 50 years. His family had obviously mourned him but like a lot of people, just could not afford to come here. It was an honour to be able to do this for them all. The feeling I had is hard to describe and although I never knew this man, the tears were streaming down my face. My heart was beating very fast and I wanted to tell everybody at home NOW that I had found him, but of course I could not. The excitement and emotion of finding him was so great, that I nearly missed hearing one of the cemetery workers asking me to follow him. He led me to the grave which was near a large tree and the gold inscription read :

5955490 PRIVATE
P R MADDAMS
The Bedfordshire and
Hertfordshire Regiment
25 August 1943 – Aged 24

At the going down of the sun and in
the Morning, we will remember him.
At Rest.

Above this Epitaph of Percy Maddams was the Insignia of the Beds & Herts Regiment and on the left a gold cross. I have found out since from my research that his death was due to Cerebral Malaria and Beri-Beri which was caused by lack of food. This case was just one in thousands. The heartache their families must have gone through must have been unbearable. No wonder the men who survived their ordeal cannot forgive their captors. Why were they all more or less starved? Why were they refused medical attention and supplies which were theirs? And why were they beaten and tortured by their Japanese captors? The only answer, I feel, is that most of the Japanese at that time were sub-human beings. From what I know and have learnt about the treatment of the POWs in the Far East I could not forgive them either.

I knelt down and placed the flowers, pink roses, which I had bought for this man, at the front of his stone. Like my Uncle, the only flowers he would have had in almost 50 years. Looking around me I had a great feeling of sadness and only hoped they were all now reunited with each other and their loved ones in that place we only know as Heaven.

After composing myself, I took photographs of Percy R Maddams' grave with the pretty pink roses at the front of it. Whilst I was doing so, ex-POW Jimmy Smith wandered over to take a photograph of me at this man's grave. Little did I know then that this photograph would be appearing in my local paper. I was so moved at finding this grave. It was as if I had done something for this man and I had not even known him, I had found him after 50 years.

A lot of the others found friends who had died but the saddest of them all was when Sylvia, another ex-POW's daughter, found her father's grave. He had been in his early thirties when he died and she could only just remember him.

Sylvia had only been 4 or 5 years old when he had left for the Far East. He, like my uncle had served with the Royal Artillery and had died in 1943 like most of the men in this Cemetery. She was obviously very upset, but happy, that she had found for the very first time the grave of her father. She had done what she had come to do. We were all so very friendly by this time that we knew how each other was feeling and that was medication in itself. Sylvia told us that now she understood things she had never understood before, and we all knew what she meant.

There were a lot of graves of men who had served with the 18th Division here, but also many graves of men from other British Regiments. Australian, Dutch, men who had served with the Indian Army, they were all here – united in death, all were our Allies. They all gave their TODAY for our TOMORROW and it must never be forgotten.

The BBC were filming here at the cemetery and were following ex-POW Jim Hill. He was looking for some of his mates he had lost from the Argyle Regiment. Unfortunately, he found none here at Kanchanaburi and thought that they may have been either cremated due to the Cholera epidemics at the camp and are honoured on the memorial walls of a different cemetery or may have a grave further up the line. Jim knew they had been here with him at some point but the

Japanese being what they were, liked to split work parties up at times to reduce the men's morale to an even lower state.

Some men were parted from their mates for periods at a time and were again united if they were lucky enough to be sent back to the same campsite. Others may not have seen their mates again until the end of the war. Sadly, a lot of these men who were parted from their friends never saw them again. Bert Miller was one of these men. He never saw his friend again, and that was one of the reasons he was here. Bert was walking around the gravestones with Jim trying to help him find at least one of his mates, but it was not to be. Jim was very disappointed and we all felt for him, but he soon cheered up because that was the sort of chap he was. He knelt down and read one particular gravestone, placed his flowers on the ground and said, "We were all prisoners together, so these will do for you just as well and sorry you did not get home." We all found we were crying for each other. We were crying for the unnecessary lost lives of all these men. It seemed as we were standing here that it might only have been yesterday that all these men had suffered and died, it certainly brought it home to you. We were all feeling so much emotion in different ways and by now a strong emotional bond was forming between us all.

I paid my last respects to Percy Maddams and had a last look around. I took a few photographs of some of the Beds &

Herts graves for my local newspaper in the hope that someone may recognise a name.

On my way back to the coach I bought a few postcards and was admiring the oriental painting of a young Thai lad. I asked him "How much?" He answered "500 baht". That was a bit expensive for me so I offered him a lower price. He spoke a little English and I explained to him that I was here on a Pilgrimage and that my father had been a Japanese POW. Without any ado he said to me, "You want, you have free". I could not believe it as somebody had told me that the Thai people usually try to get as much as they can out of the tourists. Well that made it even more special and whatever I offered him he would not accept it. It certainly would be a special memento of my visit to Kanchanaburi Cemetery. I have since had it framed and it hangs in my living room to be treasured for ever as a reminder of all those men, may be even friends of my Dad who lay in that cemetery in Kanburi.

About 100 yards away was a Chinese Cemetery. These were different gravestones to what we know. They are rounded and womb shaped, the reason for this being, that when a Chinese dies, he goes back to the womb to be reborn and every 20 years the bones are washed by a family member. There were a lot of Chinese people killed and murdered by the Japanese during the war, men, women and children. When Singapore fell and the Japanese had taken control of the Island a large group of Chinese, men, women and children were all roped together and shot on Changi beach, hundreds of them. As far as I know only two people escaped to tell the tale. The Chinese, Malay and Indian people were treated worse than the POWs although it is hard to believe it possible, but they were. Some Japanese would not think twice about torturing and killing anyone of these people. It was fun to them to ridicule and torture. When they got fed up with that, they would tie the poor unfortunates hands behind their back and behead them. They must have indeed been inhumane.

There had been a few humane Japanese who felt sadness at what was happening – one or two of the POWs had told us this – but I do not think there were many. The Japanese could be just as cruel to their own men. When an order was given, what ever it may be, woe betide any Japanese who did not carry it out.

Although the Japanese were a cruel, fanatical race, they would not think twice about dying for their Emperor. To face death and to die was an honour so, I suppose, however fanatical they were, one has to admit that they were brave and formidable fighters – eg, the kamikaze pilots. What I cannot and will never understand is why the Japanese honoured dead POWs but would enjoy inflicting tortures on live ones – it seems their whole culture at the time was evil.

I think the younger generations of Japanese have changed since the war but until they realise what their forefathers did, and until the Japanese Goverment publicly apologises for past cruelties, they will never be totally accepted.

THE RIVER KWAI

Once more we were sitting on our seats in the coach with a nice cool drink heading for the River Kwai (which during the war was the Mae Klong River). The point where the railway crossed the Mae Klong was called Tamarkan. The river was renamed the Kwai Yai in 1960. The prison camp here was known to the POWs as Tamarkan. Their job in this camp was to build the original bridge over the River Kwai, which was a small wooden one. The prisoners had to work very hard, banging heavy wooden supports into the riverbed before the actual bridge was built. There was also danger of contracting diseases from the water which a lot of them did. All drinking water needed to be boiled. A lot of men drowned due to exhaustion and if they swam to the shore they would get a beating or worse. No doubt these camps were hell on earth. This wooden bridge was bombed by the Americans, so a new steel one with concrete supports had to be erected. Work on this bridge was even more arduous. A great many men lost fingers, toes and limbs working on this bridge and of course a great many died.

We were now driving into the countryside and could see paddy fields, the first I had seen. I could remember my Dad telling me about them on his rare chats about the Far East. He used to tell me how lovely the countryside would have been if it had not have been for the fact of him being a prisoner. He also mentioned the beautiful sunsets and sunrises. I was definitely going to have to see one of those. It was like being in a different world out here. The pace was so slow and to me seeing these people working in the fields and paddy fields it could still have been the 1940's. It felt like we had gone back in time. Farming was the main way of life here in the North, unless you were fortunate enough to have a little gift shop or cafe and there were not many of those.

We had now reached the River Kwai and we all stepped from the coach. There was a short distance to walk before we came to the Bridge and River. When I saw it, although it was a very beautiful sight, the first thought that came into my head was 'how beautiful, yet so ugly'. Of course, the scene in front of me was beautiful, but it would not have been in the least beautiful to my poor old Dad and those unfortunate men who had been slaves here. I could imagine them all working so very hard, all thin and hungry, wearing only a loin cloth, some being beaten for not working hard enough and others just giving up and laying down to die. I could imagine the Japanese guards standing over them, hitting them when they thought they needed it with the usual bamboo pole or rifle butt. I can remember my Dad telling me that all the prisoners used to make jokes, swear a bit and sing rude songs. The Japanese did not realise they were swearing and laughing at them which of course caused a lot of merriment amongst the men and kept them going. From what I know and from what my Dad had told me, most of the men who did get through that 3½ years of hell, did it by willing themselves not to be beaten by the Japanese. Hate also played a great part. On the whole it was sheer luck -but unfortunately a lot of the men ran out of it.

The only thing that was an eyesore was the excavating that was going on. Most of us felt it was a shame to spoil it all for the sake of tourism. I suppose the trouble was that there was only one Hotel here near the Kwai and that was the River Kwai Village Hotel, which we were going to be staying at for the next four days. It was situated deep in the jungle.

We all found it quite repulsive to think people would be cashing in on all the men who had died here at Tamarkan. No doubt some of their remains will be dug up in the process, as it was impossible to recover all the bodies of the men killed. Many still lay somewhere in the jungle.

The weather conditions here at the Kwai were slightly different from Bangkok. Being near the river and the jungle there was a welcome breeze and although it was still humid the air was not quite so dry. We had been warned before leaving Bangkok that our clothes would be damp on opening our cases, due to this change in climate. I started walking towards the famous bridge over the River Kwai with the Railway running across it and had the same old emotional feeling come over me when stepping onto it. To my left the river was very wide, and shortly we would all be taking a barge trip up river to visit Chungkai Cemetery which during the war would have been Chungkai Prison Camp. My father had been here amongst all the other prisoners and my trip was getting more emotional as time went on. To my right the river narrowed and wound to the left.

The trees and bushes grew very thickly across the other side of the river, and it seemed to me that nothing much could have changed here. Just below the bridge floated a Restaurant made from straw and bamboo with barges tied nearby. With the sun shining down on the river it was a brilliant blue. I walked about half way across the bridge. Looking to my left again, where all those years ago the prison camp site would have been, stood the River Kwai Cafe overlooking the River. There were a great many floating houses and barges with Thai children splashing about in the water or sitting on the edge of their barge dipping their feet into it. It was indeed a precious moment standing here. My father along with his mates had had to do repairs to this bridge after the American planes had damaged the middle part.

All in all there were eleven oval spans to the bridge, which had been brought over by the Japanese from Indonesia in sections each measuring 22 metres. Due to the bombing there were only eight original spans left with two 33 metre flatter ones in the middle. Many prisoners died due to these bombing raids because the pilots were not sure of the whereabouts of the prison camp sites. Japanese soldiers were also killed, but at least they had the strength to run. It was imperative that the building of the bridges and railway was disrupted to stop the Japanese Imperial Army from transporting arms and ammunition into Burma. There are only parts of the original railway left now, which is only of historical interest – but from Kanchanaburi to Wampo you can still ride the 30 miles 3rd class which we will definitely be doing whilst we are here.

After having a last look from the bridge I started walking back towards the Kwai Cafe where all the others were. I was ready by now for a nice cool drink, which was greatly appreciated. We were all sitting at tables eating our lunch and taking in all the glorious scenery. The BBC were going to be filming all the prison camp sites and cemeteries and Philip Sherwell from the *Daily Telegraph* was asking everyone lots of questions, especially the POWs who had been out here.

There was a little market alongside the cafe so I bought a few souvenirs. Whilst doing so I overheard an American gentlemen saying that he had been one of the men who had bombed the bridge in 1943. Of course I had to have a word with him. His name was Bill Henderson. He was here on a trip with his wife and some friends. We were all so surprised at the coincidence of us all being here at the same time. Another photograph was in order.

It was almost time to head for Chungkai Cemetery and prison camp site. To do this we had to go down some steps to the motor barges that were to take us. On the way I noticed a Memorial that has been erected by the Hong Kong Male Voice Choir to commemorate visits and 50th Anniversary 1942-92. It read :

In Memory of all who perished building the Thailand and Burma Railway in Japanese POW Camps and since as a result of their harsh treatment and suffering.
None of us should forget.

The first barge had gone. It was now my turn to get on along with a few of the others. Molly, Pat Heap, whose husband was buried at Chungkai, Jimmy McNaught, his late wife's father had been a POW here, Sylvia, etc, etc. The river looked even wider from the boat and it soon got up speed. It felt so cool sitting here speeding along at about 25 miles an hour. The only time I think I did not feel hot.

CHUNGKAI

Although I did not come all this way to just admire the scenery it was breathtaking. On each side of the river there were trees and bushes of every type that grow out here, especially palm trees.

Floating holiday barges were anchored close to the river banks, made from straw, leaves, bamboo and wood. Children who were dangling their feet in the water would wave as we went by. It is a scene I will always remember for its beauty. There was a spray coming up at us from the barge which was cooling. We were almost at Chungkai Cemetery now and the scenery was becoming more mountainous as the boat was gradually slowing down. It was awful to think that almost 50 years ago there were young men walking, working and dying all around here.

Chungkai Prison Camp had been a very notorious one for the ill treatment of prisoners and heavy death tolls. They had what the prisoners referred to as kennels here. It was a form of torture amongst many. They were square bamboo cages just big enough for a human body in a crouched sitting position. Depending on the crime, which was not usually very much, the prisoner would be left in the hot burning sun with water and may be a little food just out of reach. The Jap Guards poking them with bamboo, sticks and sometimes bayonets. Some prisoners would be left like this for days and some even died. My father was one of the lucky ones and got through this torture. When the men got too ill to work on the railway they were put into the Camp Hospital, which was just another hut. If a prisoner could walk or even stand the Japs would have him out working on the railway, probably never to return. Some of the Ex-POWs have told me that they would go to bed at night and in the morning someone next to them may be dead. This happened all the time. One POW told me, "It was easy to die, but it was harder to live", and I do believe that. There must have been something driving them on, the reason may be to return to tell the tale, if not for themselves for their mates.

The boat was almost at a standstill and just edging into the bank. The first boatload was already waiting for us and there was another behind. We were helped off one by one as there was an incline leading up to some steps. I kept thinking, has my Dad walked here, but no doubt as I walked that pathway to the Cemetery my feet had touched some part where his had been. He, somehow, was getting closer and closer to me in my mind. He had been gone from us all for so long now, but little things were coming back to me, things that I had not thought about for a long time. The way he laughed, things he said, most importantly, the way he was, kind and very proud of his family. He would have done and given us anything that he could. I feel that the kind of suffering he and others went through made them appreciate all the little things in life that we so readily take for granted. I was finding out a lot about him here and a lot about myself.

We were now approaching the entrance to the Cemetery. There was nothing else here except trees. It was very quiet. No birds seemed to sing here. I do not know if it was because I did not hear them, but I could not remember hearing any. The entrance to this Cemetery was similar to Kanchanaburi, white stone. There were steps leading up to it, but instead of three rounded archways, there were three square ones. It read CHUNGKAI WAR CEMETERY 1939-1945. It was just as beautiful as Kanchanaburi with lovely bushes and flowers, the only difference being that it was so tranquil. No traffic here, just jungle. As you walk through the entrance there is again a memorial in stone which reads : "THEIR NAME LIVETH FOR EVERMORE". There is a wide walkway right through the middle of the Cemetery which is completely grassed. The grass out here in the Far East is different from ours, it is shorter and thicker. Similar to Kanchanaburi there is a large white cross at the very bottom. I have no-one to find, but there are so many Beds & Herts men buried here along with men from other British Regiments and I know my Dad had to bury a lot of them.

George Carson, another of the ex-POW's who had served with the Lanarkshire Yeomanry, pointed out to me the exact location of where the Prison camp had been. It was a couple of hundred yards from the entrance to Chungkai Cemetery. Like Kanchanaburi there were hundreds of gravestones of the same description, all grey stone, or slate with gold inscriptions and insignias. It seemed to me that a lot more men died here at Chungkai from the Beds & Herts Regiment than at Kanchanaburi. There were graves of men from all the other British Regiments. Such an unnecessary waste. War is one thing but to die as prisoners on such a large scale was unforgivable. For the men who lived and died out here, their War should have been over, but in fact, they all had to fight even harder to stay alive.

As I was walking around taking more photographs of Beds & Herts graves for my local paper, I saw Pat Heap, who was from Lancashire, standing at her husband's grave. She had just put her flowers down and I could see she was treasuring a few quiet moments alone with him. It was her second or third trip out here and she had not remarried since her husband's death here at Chungkai. She had had two sons before her husband had left for the Far East and only one of them remembered him. It was very sad seeing her standing there not wanting to leave. I asked if she wanted me to take a photograph of her standing at his grave, which she did and told me that when I sent it to her she would give it to her son. Her camera unfortunately was not working too well. The BBC were also filming here and would be doing so at all the Prison Camp sites further up the line.

On leaving I could not get over how quiet it had been here at Chungkai. At all the other places we had visited you heard birds singing and the occasional chatter of the monkeys. The Cemeteries we had seen had been as beautiful as this one, but Chungkai to me was the most peaceful.

JEATH MUSEUM

Our next stop before arriving at the River Kwai Hotel was to be the Jeath Museum, which is an open air Museum. It's structure is also a realistic construction of an actual POW's hut. It was established in 1977 by the present Chief Abbot of Wat Chaichumpol, Ven. Phra, Theppanyasuthee. This museum is now run by the Temple.

The Jeath Museum was established to collect the various items concerned with the construction of the Death Railway by the Prisoners of War. It's name is derived from J – Japan, E – England, A – America and Australia, T – Thailand, and H – Holland. Men who were prisoners of war from these countries – except, of course, Japan – were used as slave labour on the 415 kilometres of the railway. Thailand was a neutral country during the war but the Thai people suffered at the hands of the Japanese nonetheless.

The first thing you see on arriving at the museum is the bamboo hut with a collection of photographs and written articles. There are also paintings and drawings exhibited which relate to the suffering of prisoners of war, some painted by prisoners depicting the terrible things that happened in the camps which may have been the only possible way they had of expressing themselves. These paintings and drawings were very upsetting, but I felt glad that people would now know the kind of suffering that these men went through. It was bad enough for a prisoner to suffer or die himself, but to see others being tortured or killed, and knowing that they could do nothing to help, must have been unbearable mentally. The tortures used must have been conjured up by sadists. One picture depicted a man with barbed wire wound all the way around his body with Japanese Guards jumping up and down on top of him. Another showed a man being held down while his hands were bashed to a pulp with a mallet.

Some of the paintings were of Sonkurai No. 2 Camp, Chungkai and Tarso. I have never felt hate in my life for anyone, but I was coming pretty close to it now. I know justice was done in a lot of cases, but there were still a great many Japanese guilty of terrible crimes who did not pay the price. To me justice could never be done for these men who suffered and died out here in the Far East.

There were blown up photographs of men from the different camps. All were walking skeletons. There were photographs of trains and wagons the prisoners had to ride in. Group photographs of Japanese officers smiling which I found repulsive. Some of the paintings of what went on depicted things so barbaric that I could not put them down on paper.

There was another hut opposite this main hut which contained items such as pistols, knives, helmets, water canteens, etc. which had been used by POWs. There was also a large bomb which had been dropped to destroy the Kwai Bridge. This was definitely the most upsetting place that I had visited so far, but it certainly told the story. These prisoners built by force a railway in fifteen months which was predicted to take five years. Work began in June 1942 and was completed in October 1943.

We were again driving through the beautiful Thai countryside. Palm trees, banana plantations and paddy fields all flew past the coach windows. Small farms with attap type houses on stilts could be seen. There was one thing for certain, I would never see all this again. Children running about with hardly anything on, barefoot. There was no traffic on these roads, only the occasional scooter or old moped. We did see an old Army jeep or two full of young lads. Conscription was still in force out here, but other than these we were the only ones using the road. I saw my first herd of water buffalo on this road and the coach had to slow down quite a bit. We seemed to be going uphill now and the jungle was thick around us.

Suddenly the coach turned off the main road and instead of going up, we were going down, down, down. Trees and flowers were growing in abundance and the River Kwai Hotel was coming into view. It looked so pretty and was a chalet type hotel, not posh like the other hotels we had stayed at but suited this location perfectly and I knew I would really feel at home here in the days to come and also felt very close to my Dad. This was more like the way the POWs would have known Siam – no hotel, just thick jungle surrounding them for miles. It was the right setting here for our coming journey which would take us along the railway and prison camp sites.

We were now walking up towards the entrance to the hotel. Beautiful shrubs and trees of different greens and yellows surrounded it. I could never describe, however, hard I tried, the beauty of this country. The hotel was small compared to the others we had stayed at. I suppose there was not much need for large hotels, but going by what was happening at the River Kwai, things would probably change here also. It all seemed a terrible shame to me. I was now walking towards the entrance when I spotted a minah bird in a cage. A feeling of sadness suddenly came over me because my Dad always wanted one of these, and if he had lived a longer life he would have had one as well. We were all handed our keys and were led to our rooms. On opening our cases Rita and I could not believe it, steam was coming up at us. I laid all my clothes out to dry as they were quite damp due to the change of atmosphere here and hopefully the creases would come out as well.

We were all in for a dinner and Thai dancing girls again tonight so I had a nice cool shower, got dressed and went in search of the others and to have a look around. It was like a miniature jungle walking through the different pathways leading to and from the Hotel. Trees of all descriptions and flowers of every colour and hue surrounded you. Little wooden bridges led to different parts of the hotel and the hotel's pet was a tame old toucan. He did not budge an inch when you walked by him. The path I was taking at this time led to the swimming pool area. I could not believe the sight of it all. Ice blue water with palm trees, banana trees, mango trees, you name it, they had it here. A waterfall could be seen in the rocks cascading down towards the pool. It was indeed a beautiful sight and a very welcome one as well. I would definitely be taking advantage of it at every available opportunity. I started to make my way back to the Hotel Restaurant as it was almost time for dinner.

I was going to be lucky tonight because we were all going to have an English meal. I was really getting fed up with rice by now. By the time we took our seats the dancing girls were well away. They were all dressed in white oriental dresses and headgear with gold jewels adorning them. The stage was at one end of the Restaurant with an open air balcony running all the way around the Hotel. All you could see were trees, bushes and flowers all around you and surrounding these was the jungle. I suddenly saw something move on the wall; it was a lizard. In fact, lizards were crawling all over the walls. I did not mind them as long as they did not jump or bite. Mabel and Hilda, two widows of ex-POWs were not so keen on them though and every now and then would make sure they were still where they should be, on the wall.

By now our meals were on the table and I thoroughly enjoyed it, and savoured every mouthful as it would probably be rice again tomorrow. The usual fruits were to be had for afters and I then sat and chatted to ex-POW Bert Miller and his son-in-law before retiring to the bar with everyone. They were holding a disco for us tonight so we would all be having a bit of fun. A few of us started to dance and Ron our Thai guide pulled little old Daisy up, 83 years of age, and started dancing with her. It was lovely to see her enjoying herself as we all did.

After a while we had to sit down as it was so hot. We certainly had a lot to drink that evening, especially Linda, and we also had a good night's sleep. Before going to bed I walked down to the edge of the river. All you could hear was the sound of the crickets and frogs. It was so peaceful. Just in case my Dad was listening I told him that I was here just for him.

The Death Railway

Today we were heading for what was left of the usable railway which runs from Kanchanaburi to Wampo and were to take a 3rd class journey along the 30 miles of railway which remains in operation. This part of the railway is mainly used to attract the tourists. It did not take us long to get to the station at Kanchanaburi and on descending from the coach could see a large sign which read 'The Trans Kwai Death Railway – Welcome To' which sounded back to front to me, but probably would not to a native of Thailand. We all walked into the station and as our train would not be coming in for about 20 minutes I started to have a look around. The first thing that I had to do was to walk on to the railway where may be my Dad had worked laying the sleepers or hammering in the nails. There were a few original sleepers left and I had to touch them. My Dad may have worked on any part of this railway and it was very important to me to do this. Perhaps only someone in a similar situation as myself would be able to understand. This railway was the main reason why the prisoners in Thailand were treated so badly. The Japanese wanted this railway quickly to transport arms, ammunition, etc into Burma and as they were an ignorant race thought that by treating the prisoners badly, by depriving them of basic human needs and by physical and mental torture that the railway would be finished sooner. If they had only realised for their own sake as well as the POWs by treating them well, the men would have been fitter with very few deaths and the railway would have been completed even more quickly or just as quickly.

Jimmy MacKay and Arthur (Mitch) Miller both POWs got down onto the railway and relived old times by picking up a piece of rock which they would have had to break up into small pieces. They seemed to get a bit emotional on doing this, but they were showing us younger ones what they had to do. We all started walking across the rails to have a look at an actual locomotive which the Japanese used to transport arms and ammunition into Burma.

Luckily, there were not many such journeys due to the Americans bombing the bridges and parts of the railway. I got up on the train with Jimmy MacKay to get a better look. This locomotive had been kept or restored very well and had been made in England. It was ironic to think that the Japanese used our own locomotives, amongst other things, in the war against us! It was now almost time to get on the train. You could just see it coming in so we all scrambled back across the rails. Ex-POW Arthur Lane and his wife Dot told us to try and get a seat on the left hand side of the train because we would have a better view when we came to Wampo bridge and viaduct.

So that was what most of us did. There was no glass in the windows, obviously because of the heat which meant we could all get some good photographs as well. The seats were made of wood, no cushioning at all. It all looked very old and once the train started to move off it felt like there was no suspension either.

Arthur pointed out to a truck on rails. It was an original truck used by the POWs for transporting rail materials further up the line. The truck would be taken to where more materials were needed. The train was still going along quite slowly, uphill and I could see just below me two large elephants at work carrying logs. I stuck my head out of the window to take a photograph.

We were told by Ron, our guide that the Thai people look after their elephants very well. When training young elephants their legs are chained together so as they do not run and endanger themselves and others. The main village to see these elephants at work is Changmai. A bit further along I could see some Thai farmers cutting crops with their scythes. It was handy not having glass in the window, it made it very easy when taking photographs. The train was gathering up speed now and all I could see were the hedgerows. I was sitting facing Molly and Sylvia, daughters of POWs like myself, but they unlike me, were unfortunate in the fact that their fathers never came home. At least I had known and loved my Dad and vice versa for 19 years of my life.

We were going along quite fast now and could feel all the bumps. Looking ahead of me through the carriage window, the rails were very uneven, probably due to the fact of the POWs having to work very fast to finish the railway. It felt wonderful, yet sad, travelling on this railway knowing that my Dad along with all the other prisoners were forced to build it. I did know one thing for sure, and that was when my Dad had been out here during his captivity, never would he have believed that I would be travelling on this railway, walking on it and touching it with my hands as his had done. My Dad had certainly been here, I could feel it.

The train was now slowing down quite a bit and we were about to cross over the River Kwai Bridge. It was going so slow that you could almost reach across and touch it. The view from the carriage window was breathtaking. The engine driver suddenly gave a few hoots to warn anyone crossing the bridge to get out of the way and we started gaining speed again.

Sylvia, Molly and I were discussing a few things to do with the war and our fathers, when all of a sudden this woman came over and sat next to me. Once she started talking I could tell she was an American. She told us that she was out here on holiday with friends. She had overheard us talking and wanted to know more. It astounded us that she never knew very much at all about the sufferings of the POWs during their captivity and did not realise how many had died until she had visited the cemeteries.

She asked us about our fathers. Molly and Sylvia told her that their fathers never got home which seemed to shock her greatly. She then asked me about my father. I showed her an old Army photograph of him, and told her that he did survive, but was never very fit after his treatment as a POW. I then showed her a photograph of my Dad aged 52, a year before he died. Again she was shocked, and although she did not say anything, I knew she thought he looked like an old man, because he did. At 52 he looked more like 75. When I look at that photograph I feel very sad as it was one of the last photographs taken of my father and although very ill, never complained and I will always admire him for his courage.

After our conversation with this American woman, who must have been about the same age as myself, early forties, she with tears in her eyes, shook us all by the hand and said that talking to us had made her holiday much more meaningful, and we could all see that she meant it.

The BBC TV cameras were very busy taking film out of the carriage windows. Linda and I were the only daughters in our party now whose fathers had got this far and further up the line. I knew from talking to my Dad's old pals who were out here with him that he had got as far as Wampo and Tarso. I could remember my Dad talking about a Camp called Nicki Nicki, a very notorious camp where a great many men died due to maltreatment, so I think he must have got as far as the Burma border. My research had shown that my Dad had definitely been held at Chungkai, Wampo and Tarso – Tarso being a large notorious camp also. Because of the POWs becoming separated at times into different working parties, they did not always know how far up the line their mates had gone or which camp they were in. Some men who became too ill to work were taken to the Camp Hospital, but you had to be unable to walk for such luxuries. Others who were still on their feet were marched, if needed, to other camps to work, usually to make up for prisoners that had died.

The train was slowing down now and Jimmy Smith and Arthur Lane pointed out to Linda and I the Chungkai cutting. Both our fathers had been here and the Prison camp and Cemetery we had visited must have been nearby. Again I felt sad looking at this cutting between the rocks, thinking that my Dad had been one of the men who had had to chisel away at it to make way for the Railway. The train only just went through and if it had stopped it would have been easy to touch the rocks. It was unbelievable seeing all this history with my own eyes and after all these years. There were drill holes still to be seen where dynamite was placed to blast the rock. It was still hard for me to take in the fact that I was out here at all. If anyone had told me six months before that I would be seeing all this I would never have believed them.

The train started chugging a bit, going slower and slower. Arthur suddenly pointed out to us a cave where two unfortunate POWs were murdered by the Japanese. They were caught having a smoke at the spot where the Japanese were going to set off a charge, so an order was purposely given to let off the charge too soon and they were killed. There is a Memorial in their honour at the exact spot.

My trip was getting more emotional by the minute. We all shed a lot of tears but even so, were all glad to be here. For the Ex-POWs in our party their main reason for being here seemed to be to lay old ghosts to rest, and us younger ones always seemed to know when they needed a bit of support or a joke or two and I really think it helped them having us here to liven things up a bit when they felt down.

As for us daughters, to be able to see for ourselves what our fathers lives were like out here and to understand things we never understood before – I for one knew already that I was going to go home with much more of my Dad than I had come with, and I could not have had anything more precious.

We were now approaching Wampo Bridge and Viaduct. We could see the river below us and Jim Smith pointed to where Wampo camp site had been, which was up river to the left. We were now looking straight down at the river, a drop of about 30 feet. The train was going along so slowly because the bridge was still supported by the original timbers. How the POWs built this against the sheer rock face was unimaginable.

We were now going around a deep curve on the viaduct which was called the death curve, the reason being that so many men died during the construction of it. To the right all you could see, a few inches from the windows of the train was sheer rock. Most of the POWs we were with had been working on this bridge along with Linda's Dad and mine. It was terrible to think of all the suffering and death that was attributed to this place called Wampo and I could now see why my father had never really been a fit man for very long like a lot of the others.

On the other side of the river, which looked a muddy brown was the jungle and Burma. A small hotel cashing in on tourism stood in the midst of trees and flowering shrubs and there were the usual floating barges along the banks.

The train now came to a stop at a sign saying Wang Po Railway Station – Saoyok, Kanchanaburi. Places out here although said and spelt differently are the same but to the POWs this was Wampo, a place they would have rather not known.

Once off the train, I walked the short distance to Wampo Bridge. Looking back on that awesome sight, especially the 'death curve', which was almost a half circle going around the sheer rock face, I could not help but wonder how all the prisoners had built it, taking into account their poor state of health. The 40 feet high timbers running along the entire length of the viaduct were supported underneath near the river bank by concrete. These timbers looked all of their 50 years and I wondered which part my Dad had worked on. I have since seen old film of Wampo showing elephants as well as men working. It must have taken a great deal of inner strength and courage and I could only feel complete sadness and total admiration for all of them. There was so much suffering and so many deaths here during the building of this barbaric construction, and we all felt that if we had not known the Prisoners had built this bridge and viaduct known as Wampo, we would never have believed it.

Linda and I both wanted to have a walk on this bridge that again our Dads had helped to build, but we had to be very careful as there were a few sleepers missing here and there.

Ex-POW George Carson pointed over to where the prison camp would once have been. He knew, as he had also been here along with most of the other POWs in our party. Shortly we would be going by boat to this camp site.

Linda and I were just walking back when Jimmy McNaught called to us. He wanted to show us a cave which had been converted into a shrine. At the same time Jim Smith shouted to us to be careful walking on the bridge as there were some quite big gaps. I had been concentrating on where I was putting my feet but as he shouted I looked over to where he was and almost stuck my foot in a hole. I had to do a quick jump, but got off the bridge in one piece, with the two Jims' and Linda having a good laugh. I never did get to see the Shrine after that!

Those of us that were able were now going to have to climb down some rocks to board a boat which would be taking us to Wampo prison camp site. It was situated up river, just past and adjacent to the bridge and viaduct. Joe, one of our party who had come on this trip just out of interest, had to help me down as there was nothing to hold on to. It was a sheer drop down if you fell. There were about fifteen of us including Alan and Alistair, the BBC cameramen.

From the river the view was totally different. We could see the complete length of the bridge and viaduct and had a very good view of all those timbers, the whole of which had caused the deaths of so many of the men. The rock or cliff face must have been at least 200 feet high and small trees and bushes grew upon it. If it had not been for the way in which this bridge had been built, it would have been a pretty sight, but I could not detach that fact from my mind.

We were now on our way to Wampo Camp site which was not very far. It took us about 5 minutes in the boat and it drew up against the riverbank to enable us all to get off without getting wet feet. There were a lot of trees growing further back but the part of the camp site that was left was about the size of a cricket pitch. The grass was very brown and dead looking here, which seemed odd being so near the river.

As soon as my feet touched the ground, I knew my Dad had been here. I could feel it. I could not explain or describe this feeling to anyone and must have been one of those inexplicable feelings a lot of us experience at one time or another during our lives. I never had this experience again during my visits to other camp sites along the railway where I knew my father had been, and although Wampo must have been a terrible place, it now held something special for me. I bent down and picked up a leaf to take home, It would always remind me of this place where my Dad had once been.

I walked the entire length width and breadth of this ground as I knew my footsteps would, and did touch his. My feelings were happy yet sad standing here and I could not stop the tears falling. George Carson who had also been here at Wampo said to me that he was walking over his own footsteps and that I would be walking over my Dads, but I already knew.

We were just about to go when we suddenly saw a train, going so slowly, back over the bridge, probably the one that had brought us here but our return journey would be by coach.

It had been an honour to ride this railway for my Dad and to visit this camp site that I would never forget.

Once again we all got onto the boat which was to return us to where we had first boarded. Hardly anyone spoke on the way back. I think we all needed a few quiet moments to ourselves after this very emotional visit. It would not be quite so bad climbing back up the rocks as it had been coming down and the coach would be there waiting for us when we arrived.

We were now on our way back to the River Kwai Hotel. It was good to just sit and do nothing after our exhausting but wonderful day. I knew where I would be going when we got back, for a lovely dip in the pool and that was just what I did along with most of the others.

Afterwards I had a nice cool shower and telephoned home which was quite expensive from the Kwai. 500 baht about £14 for 3 minutes. It was well worth it though just to hear their voices again.

That evening we all had drinks together in the bar and were told that there was a barbecue being held in the hotel grounds. So we all walked down the winding paths towards it. It was lovely being all together, letting our hair down for once which lifted our spirits in readiness for tomorrow's visits which were to be Hell Fire Pass and Kinsayok, the only prison camp site which has remained as it was 50 years ago.

For me, the most important visit tomorrow would be a specially arranged trip in the afternoon to Tarso, a once notorious prison camp which had been for my father, his main camp site. I, as it happened, was to be the only female on this trip as I was the only daughter whose father had been a POW there out of our party. I would be accompanying some of the POWs who had also spent time there.

DAY 9 – 21ST FEBRUARY

Hell Fire Pass

I felt very tired on waking this morning. My room-mate Rita had had a bad night with her stomach. A lot of the others had suffered also, but luckily whatever it was did not affect me. I was as enthusiastic as ever even though a bit tired.

We were again on our way. It was still, of course, very humid but by now our bodies had acclimatised to the heat. There was no stopping the sweat but I for one, was handling the heat a lot better.

Once out of the hotel grounds it was open countryside all the way. The further north we travelled the more mountainous was the view. It was quite beautiful and there were many herds of cattle to be seen including water buffalo.

We had only gone a few miles when the coach suddenly stopped. The reason being for us to have a look at one of the original trains used during the war for transporting rail materials up and down the line. This train had also been used for transporting troops, arms and ammunition into Burma. It was left on the rails as a reminder of all the suffering that prisoners of war went through. It looked very old, as indeed it was and was a rust brown colour. It had many trucks and carriages attached and I, along with Arthur Lane and Jimmy Mackay, had to get onto it. I have, since my trip, seen film taken during the construction of the railway, showing trains like this one with Japanese officers posing before the camera smiling widely as if they were on a day's outing. No thought at all for the men who were suffering or dying even a few feet away from them. I also remember seeing a train like this one on film taken when the war in the Far East was over, carrying ex-POWs out of Thailand.

The next stop before Hell Fire Pass was to visit a site where two original cattle wagons stood as a sort of monument on a disused part of the railway as another reminder of how the prisoners were treated. As I have said previously the men were herded 30-40 to a wagon the 1200 miles from Singapore to Bangkok with the sun burning down upon them with hardly any food or water to drink. When nature called the toilet would have been a corner of the wagon. A great many men, if they were not ill already, were when they arrived at their destination, or worse. A shiver ran through me imagining it all. It was heartrending to think that thousands of men including my Dad had been herded like cattle onto one of these wagons.

We only had a short distance to travel now, which would bring us to Hell Fire Pass.

This part of the railway came to be known as 'Hell Fire Pass' to the POWs because they had to work through the night as well as the day by torchlight. A Padre who was also a POW was known to have said that 'It was like looking down on the Fires of Hell.'

Because of the men having to work much longer hours, due to the Japanese wanting the Railway finished more quickly, Speedo Sessions were introduced. The POWs would have to work 18-20 hours a day with the Japanese Guards pushing, prodding and beating them saying 'Speedo, Speedo'. That is how these sessions came to be known as 'Speedo Sessions' to the prisoners. Ex-POW Jimmy MacKay had been here and had told me that when one prisoner went back to camp, another would be sent out to work, like a sort of rota system, the only trouble being that on returning to camp, each prisoner did not know who he would find dead or alive. Some never returned and are to this day buried somewhere near to where they died working on that railway. To the Japanese death was an honour and to be a prisoner was shameful, so however many men died, it meant nothing to them as long as the railway was completed on time. What a way to die: starved, diseased, tortured and worked to death. It is a terrible thing to have to say, but to many it was easier to die; it was staying alive that was hard.

There were a great many Australians working on this part of the Railway, but also men from all the different Regiments. Most ex-POWs from our party had toiled here also, and would be seeing it once again. I did not know whether my father had been here, but he could have been. These Speedo Sessions that the men had to endure caused a much greater death toll and by this time the men were so emaciated that most of them could not withstand the strain and treatment received from their captors. Many Australian POWs died here along with men of other races and from other Regiments.

The coach had once again stopped and those of us that could manage it were going to climb down quite a few steps which would take us to Hell Fire Pass. At least there were some railings to hold on to and it looked as if there were about 100 steps. Going down would be easy but coming back up would definitely be hard work, especially in this heat and no doubt I would be once again saturated with sweat. But that was not going to stop me.

At last I got to the bottom following ex-POW Arthur Lane, his wife Dot and daughter Glenys. We had about a quarter of a mile to walk before we reached the pass, but on walking, the odd bit of rail or sleeper could be seen. It was very dry and humid and the trees and bushes were brown and dead looking. The odd bit of greenery could be seen here and there. It seemed as if we had been transported all of a sudden from Summer into Autumn. There were some funny looking pods on the ground, so I picked a couple up to take home as another reminder of my trip. I did try to grow one but it did not work out, but stuck the other one in my scrapbook.

Looking around me to my left I saw a sheer drop, overgrown with trees and bushes all of a brown colour; to my right the mountainous rock going upwards. We had to be very careful when walking as there were sticks and bits of wood sticking up out of the ground. As we neared the pass, we could see the rails and sleepers very clearly. The wooden sleepers looked very old and were rotten. This was definitely part of the original railway, nothing had been replaced here.

I was actually now looking at the cutting through the rocks which gave it's name to Hell Fire Pass which was about 50 feet high. The rock had been blasted with dynamite, drilled and chiselled away to form a pass. It must have been treacherous work for the POWs. They would have had to clear all the rock away before being able to start work on the actual railway and the suffering and death on these 'Speedo Sessions; must have been so great. We were all probably standing on a spot where some poor man had died, and the POWs amongst us were covering the same ground where once they had been walking skeletons.

The BBC cameramen were taking a lot of film here and any one of us could see that even they were becoming quite emotional at some of the sights they were seeing. The Japanese certainly did need a whole Army for what they had in store. What a terrible shame that the whole Army did not get home, or even half of them come to that. The Japanese definitely have a lot to answer for.

On one side of the pass, adhered to the rock, was a memorial in gold in honour of all the men who died here. The Australians had also laid a memorial on part of the railway to their comrades who had died at this terrible place. There were also a few wreaths lying against the rock face.

Some Japanese veterans had also been here, as they had left some sort of scrolls which opened up. We were told by Ron, our Thai Guide, that Japanese war veterans often come here to pay penance for what happened during the construction of the Railway. I suppose they think that this forgives them their sins, although I did not think so at all and neither did anybody else. At one point we did have to pass some Japanese veterans who may have taken part in the atrocities, and it was quite noticeable that the ex-POWs kept well away. Seeing them must have brought back some terrible memories.

We were now going to have to make our way back to the coach and climb up those steep stone steps which would most certainly take a lot longer than it did coming down.

KINSAIYOK

The last coach stop of the morning before going back to the Kwai Hotel for lunch was to be our visit to Kinsaiyok POW Camp Site. This site has been kept almost as it had been all those 50 years ago. Obviously wood, bamboo, leaves, etc. would have been replaced as such things deteriorate quite quickly due to the heat and humidity.

The sun was very hot now as we stepped from the coach. We had not noticed it so much at Hell Fire Pass because we had been shaded by trees. It was more open here with signposts in various languages including English showing you which way to go.

I did not know if my Dad had been here, but I have a feeling he had, because I can remember him mentioning to me that very occasionally the Jap Guards would let the prisoners bathe in the water. Going by what ex-POW Arthur had told me the water here was the only clean water to be had during their captivity.

To me this camp site was kept much better than it would have looked during the POWs time out here. I suppose for the tourist's benefit.

There were different paths to take. One led to the original camp site, a second to an original suspension bridge built by POWs. A third led to an original Japanese Stove and the fourth took you to the Saiyok Waterfall. Nearby was an Attap Hut, although not an original, the same sort of hut the prisoners would have had to live in after building it themselves.

The first path some of us took including myself, was to the actual prison camp site. It was a very large area with trees growing here and there, some looking quite dead. I could not see much bamboo growing around this site, but during their captivity the POWs would have had to cut most of it down for the building of their attap huts etc.

It was very sad imagining all those young men working, suffering and a lot dying around here which was what happened at all the camps. The earth looked very sandy and red and surrounding the dead looking trees were healthy green ones. Ex-POW Jim Smith noticed to the side of us a look out post almost hiding between the trees. We had been told it was an original except for the supports. It felt very eerie looking up at it trying to imagine a Japanese Guard looking down.

Next I decided to take a look at the Japanese Stove. It was built on a concrete slab. It's size was about 20 x 7 feet with wooden railings all around it just high enough to lean your elbows upon. It had a tiled outer roof with wooden beams underneath, but during the war would have been made from bamboo and leaves to give protection against the rains so that the coals would not go out and to stop the food from becoming wet. The Japanese must certainly have made sure that they had enough food to eat, but I doubt whether any POW would have eaten anything cooked on that stove. All they got was a cupful of rice which was unfit for human consumption let alone the maggots and weevils that lived in it. To spice it up they sometimes had onion water.

Next on the agenda was the Waterfall. As our Dads may have been here, Linda and I left the others and followed the sign. The scenery was very pretty as we walked on, but somehow wherever we were on our travels it was never fully appreciated due to what we knew happened here in the Far East. As we neared the Saiyok waterfall we saw a very large rock with water cascading down. This, we were told by Ron our Thai guide, was the bathing area which no-one but the Japanese officers occupied.

The waterfall was quite beautiful and surrounded by trees. It was the clearest water I had seen since arriving in the Far East. It carried on into many little rivulets running here and there over the rocks and between trees and bushes, then slightly downhill into a large steam. It was not very deep at all so Linda and I took off our sandals and stepped into the water. We had to be very careful as the rocks were very slippery and uneven. The depth of the water only reached to just below our knees and felt very refreshing. We paddled out as far as we dared and it felt good once again to think that may be we were paddling where our Dads had once paddled or bathed all those years ago.

Unfortunately, I never did get to see the Suspension Bridge as time ran out and the coach was waiting to take us all back to have lunch at the River Kwai Hotel.

TARSO

Whilst most of the others were going for a dip in the Tropical Pool, I, along with seven others were going to visit what remained of Tarso prison Camp site which was a specially arranged trip. Tarso, now known as Nam Tok had been excluded from the Itinerary mainly because much of the once camp site was now under water due to flooding. Nevertheless, those of us that had a special interest in the site still wanted to go.

My reasons, of course, being that Tarso had been one of my Dad's main camp sites and I felt that I could not miss out on seeing what I could of it after coming all this way. The others felt the same. I was to be the only female and the only one of our group of relatives of POWs whose father had been held captive there. I would be accompanying former POWs Jim Hill, Jim Smith, George Carson and Bert Miller. Bert's son-in-law also wanted to go as did two others from our party, solely out of interest.

TARSO had been a very large notorious Prison camp, well known for the ill treatment of prisoners. This part of Thailand during the war had been very rough jungle and before starting work on the railway, the prisoners would have had to clear it. My father had been one of these men. Prisoners, many from the 18th Division were marched 80 miles to this camp with only a few meals of soggy rice and watery stew, ending up completely exhausted. A great many deaths were attributed to this march and most of them suffering from dysentery, malaria or both.

The prisoners that were too sick to work would build the living quarters, attap huts made from bamboo and attap leaves. Men were dying every day due to workload, disease and malnutrition caused by near starvation. The dead were sewn up in rice bags and buried. The graves were numbered and marked by a wooden cross with name, number and

Regiment upon them. But as death became commonplace in all the camps, communal graves, especially during the cholera epidemics had to come into force. Cholera became rife in all the camps at one time or another. Most POWs who contracted Cholera died within a short period. Very few got over it.

Tropical ulcers were very common, especially when clearing the jungle. Many men had to have limbs amputated, usually their legs due to gangrene setting in and a man thought himself very lucky if any form of anaesthetic was available, which it usually was not. The Japanese could have helped a lot of these men, but refused to hand over any form of medication. It is very sad to think even now that a lot of those men went through all that hell, yet still died.

Further on from Tarso was another camp called Tonchan. Tonchan had been another main camp of my fathers, but due to flooding nothing now remained of it.

It was a very hot afternoon and Ron our Guide was joining us to help find the way. Everything looked so different since the war to the Ex-POW's but with Ron's help we were hoping to find what remained of Tarso.

Only a few of us this time boarded the coach and we started on our way eating dried banana sweets which Ron offered us. He looked after us very well and was also very entertaining. He told us what we could eat and what we could not eat as our stomachs were more sensitive than the Thai peoples. So if Ron told us not to eat a certain thing, we did not.

We were going along a dusty road now and coming into a small village. All the houses were wooden shacks or houses on stilts with spirit houses outside most of them. The easiest way to describe a spirit house would be to say that it looked more like a bird table but with a small pagoda sitting on the top. These spirit houses are very sacred, and a native of Thailand, when passing by, would show respect with some sort of acknowledgement, like a nod of the head or a hoot if driving. Ron told us that every time a member of the family died a spirit house would be erected to keep the deceased's spirit alive and also to keep evil spirits away.

The coach finally stopped at the end of the dusty road and it looked as though we were going to have to walk the rest of the way. The veterans amongst us seemed to remember that the river was nearby, also the railway lines so I just followed them all. There was only one small dusty roadway leading off to the left from the main one with shacks on both sides, some made from straw, leaves and bamboo, others from wood with corrugated iron rooves. We could tell it was a very poor area, and had not changed much since the war. My Ex-POW friends were trying to get their bearings and decided to turn right at an opening between two worn down empty shacks. It was all open ground and as we walked on came to the railway track. The sleepers were very worn. Before coming out to the Far East I never thought that a railway track would bring so much sadness to a person looking on them, but these did. All the POWs I was with had worked on this part of the railway and it must have brought some terrible memories back to them. They shed the odd tear now and again and I felt sad for them all. Yet for some reason, they told me it made them feel better and that old ghosts were laid to rest. My father could have worked anywhere around here and I might have been treading in his footsteps once again.

Walking away from the tracks and on a bit further we passed fields where sugar cane was being gathered in and I saw my first banana plantation, which was very educational for me because I had always thought that bananas grew downwards not upwards. At this point my elderly friends seemed to remember the ground they were walking. Bert thought the river would be nearby and almost as soon as he spoke a small wooden bridge came into view. On the left of the bridge you were able to walk down to the river's edge where covered in barges were anchored. To the right of the bridge the river came up to the banks and Thai children were playing and splashing about on a bamboo raft that was near a bamboo house boat. I was told by the others that the prison camp would have been a few miles up river to the right, but unfortunately, we could not go any further. We all walked away from the bridge and started walking down to the river's edge. This brought back vivid memories to the former POWs and they told me that the boats carrying rice would stop here and the prisoners would be made to take it back to camp usually pushing sacks of it in some sort of cart. Bert thought Tarso camp site would have been about six miles from here, and by the time they had got there with the sacks of rice, they were too worn out to eat it.

This part of the river had not changed at all either since the war so I was told. There was less ground due to the flooding but the rest had been untouched.

On walking back we all noticed an opening through the Banana Plantation. Those that had been here remembered it as being the track used for transporting the rice to Tarso.

It must have been a very strange feeling for my friends to be able to retrace their steps after all these years and perhaps I my fathers.

On leaving I picked up a banana leaf as another reminder that my Dad had once been here at this place known as Tarso.

Before we got back onto the coach we all had a look around at some market stalls that we had not noticed on our arrival. I saw some ice lollies for sale and was just about to buy one, when Ron stopped me by saying, 'You, no allowed'. So that was that. Back on the coach I went and had a drink instead.

I felt completely worn out. The walking and the heat had certainly got to me, and I was the youngest on this outing. The others would definitely be feeling it, but as all of us agreed, it had been well worth it.

On arriving back at the hotel I changed into my bathing costume and jumped straight into the welcoming tropical pool. I just lay there floating on my back, relaxing and thinking over the emotional events of the day.

That evening after dinner, we all had a bit of a do and by now were one big happy family. How we got up early every morning was incredible after our very late nights, but we all managed and dozed when we could on the coach.

Tomorrow was to be our last trip visiting prison camp sites, which would take us as far as the Burma border.

Kuri Konta and Konkuita

The BBC team had left us now, but today was for the rest of us, the last day at the River Kwai Hotel and our visits to the prison camp sites would come to an end.

On reaching Three Pagoda Pass we will have travelled the complete length of the Railway from Bangkok in Thailand to the Burma border which measures 295 kilometres. Passes at present were not being given to enable anyone to cross the Burma line. What I had seen so far of my Dad's life out here had left it's mark and I would never forget any of it. I do not suppose I will ever find out for sure how far he did get working on that railway.

Our first stop of the day was to visit what was left of Kuri Konta and Konkuita Prison Camp sites. It was at Konkuita where Thai and Burma teams met on completion of the railway on the 17 October 1943. It was said that a golden nail was hammered in by the Japanese as part of a Ceremony held on the 25 October 1943 in honour of their Emperor Hirohito. Prisoners of war had to attend also.

Feelings were mixed about what completion of the railway meant to the POWs. On the one hand they were thankful to think that the long hours of slave labour and speedo sessions were over and hopefully, tasks of road-building, woodcutting, etc would become lighter. Large hospitals (attap huts) were set up where the more emaciated POWs could recover from their ordeals. On the other hand, the fittest men were sent to Japan to work in the mines on unmarked cargo ships, often to be sunk by Allied submarines and aircraft, my Uncle being one of these unfortunate men. For the POWs who did end up working in the mines of Japan, treatment was very harsh. Comparing the work in the mines to work on the Burma Railway, they were totally different. Instead of the intense heat working in Thailand on the railway the mine workers had to contend with the freezing cold and a great many died through severe frostbite. Be it the railway or the mines the men were tortured, starved and died just the same.

Now the railway was finished it also meant that the Japanese would now transport troops, arms and ammunition into Burma. This was not good, so it was up to the POWs to sabotage parts of the railway whenever they could, with a lot of help from American and RAF bomber aircraft. Now, instead of building the railway, groups of men were sent out to repair the bridges and track. At the same time they did their best to damage some other part if they possibly could. The only trouble with that was when repairs had been done, the POWs were often made to test certain parts out before the Japanese were satisfied that it was safe.

The Kwai Bridge and the Bridge and Viaduct at Wampo were on many occasions damaged, especially by the Americans dropping bombs, which unfortunately killed a lot of prisoners as well. It was imperative that damage to the railway and bridges went ahead. Thankfully, the Japanese only used the railway a few times before it was unusable again.

When you think of all the torture the prisoners went through, it was all for nothing. The railway was never used again after the war. The rails were removed and the wooden sleepers rotted away. Only in places can you see original parts of the railway track that was left untouched except of course the track used between Kanchanaburi and Wampo for the purpose of tourism.

The coach had travelled some distance already, countryside all the way. The further north we went the more mountainous the view.

We were now slowing down and the coach pulled up onto a grass verge. For as far as we could see, the view in front of us was all that was left of Kuri Konta and Konkuita prison camp sites. Similar to Tarso these sites, which had once been valleys were now under water due to flooding from the

Brankassi Dam, which was about 36 kilometres south of Konkuita. There were small bushes growing here and there, but other than these, all that could be seen were the tops of dead trees sticking out of the water. It was a very desolate-looking place, except for one floating barge in the middle of this man-made lake. I wondered how many men still lay out there. I could only just see the tops of the hills at the other side of the water as there was quite a bit of mist. Some POWs in our party remembered this place only too well and went very quiet indeed. These prison camps further north were the worst to have worked and survive in. You were counted as one of the lucky ones if you got no further than Tamarkan (River Kwai) and that was bad enough. This was a very sad place and I soon decided I had had enough and got back on the coach to wait for the others.

Our journey was now taking us into more hilly terrain, and we were now on our way to Three Pagoda Pass which was situated next to the Burma border.

THREE PAGODA PASS

Burma is now known as Myanmar, but I prefer to still call it Burma. That is how my Dad would have known it and the same went for me. We passed more water buffalo as we went along and could see the difference in the scenery, much more hilly than Thailand, thick with trees and bushes. It was very quiet and all the time we were going along in the coach we did not see one person. Ron, our guide, told us that the Burmese people still more or less lived as they did 50 years ago. Nothing much had changed for them and we were bound to see a few of them where we were going. They, themselves were much darker skinned than the Thai people, and a lot, especially the older ones had black teeth, due to a habit they enjoyed, chewing beetle nut. If we saw any black marks on the ground, we were told, that is what it would be, as they had to spit it out when they had finished chewing it.

From leaving the Kwai Hotel, it must have taken us about an hour, but we had finally arrived at Three Pagoda Pass. We could see from the coach the three small Temples in the centre of the village which symbolised to ex-POWs the point where the railway crossed the Thai Burma border.

The coach pulled up alongside a building which was the Tourist Police Headquarters. Their job was to stop anybody crossing the Burma line, as it was out of bounds. There was a lot of trouble going on there, something to do with Press Ganging for the building of some pipeline. It did not sound at all good to me. I do not think that any of these Military Policemen would have thought twice about shooting anyone if they had to, as they all carried rifles and pistols.

It was quite open here and very mountainous. There was only the Tourist Police Station, which was a wooden oriental looking building and a small market with the three temples situated right in the middle. These pagodas were white and about four feet high with gold around the top of them. At the bottom of each was a small opening for religious purposes I supposed.

There was roughly a six feet gap between each one and they had been fenced off with low iron railings to protect them.

Ex-POW Arthur Lane walked me over to where the outskirts of Niki Niki Camp would once have been. He told me of the brutality there and that there were not many survivors. My Dad, on his rare occasions of talking about his time in the Far East, had mentioned this camp and I am almost sure he was held captive here. Hundreds of men died at Niki which had been another camp renowned for its death toll. The Burmese people had had two memorial stones erected on this site in honour of all the prisoners that had died. The railway track ran alongside these stones.

During the war, many Thai and Burmese people helped POWs and even saved their lives, both by hiding them and giving them food and medicine, if there was any to be had.

Opposite these Memorial stones was a look-out post once used by the Japanese and had now been rebuilt and was used by the Tourist Police.

This was the only village for miles and during the war must have been all jungle except for the prison camp that had to be built.

About 100 yards opposite the Tourist Police Station was the Burma Border with a barrier stopping anyone from crossing the line. A sign was attached to the barrier which read, 'No-one is Allowed to Pass'. I could see the railway track from the barrier which came to an abrupt end a few yards past the Burma line.

Before leaving we all decided to look around the market. Here is where I bought myself a sarong. I did not know if I would ever have the chance or the nerve to wear it but I bought it anyway and some earrings for my daughter.

The Burmese people we saw were much darker skinned than the Thais. Some had very beautiful fresh looking faces with high cheek bones and big black eyes. The children and babies were adorable and all of these people seemed very laid back. Ron our guide told us that the further you went into Burma you could come across different tribes of Burmese people. Sometimes it felt to me that I was in an entirely different world from the one I knew.

It was now time to leave Three Pagoda pass. Before arriving back at the Hotel we were to stop and have our packed lunch at Sonkuri, pronounced Sonkrai, after which we were going to visit a Buddhist Temple, and some Hot Springs.

SONKURI

It was not far to Sonkuri, which turned out to be the dirtiest looking place I had seen so far on my travels. All there was at this place was a large dirty looking market with people selling their wares or dozing next to their stalls. The only reason I got out of the coach was to stretch my legs. If it was so filthy now, what must it have been like for the POWs in the camp here during the war. I had seen a photograph of three POWs at Changi Museum, Singapore taken at Sonkurai No. 1 Camp with the words 'Three Fit Workers'. The photograph showed three walking skeletons and only one of these men made it home. There were a great many POWs at this brutal camp and very few survived.

Next on the Agenda was a visit to a Buddhist Temple. The Temple was the focal point in this small village with stilt houses on each side. These houses were made from wood. The living and sleeping quarters were at the top held up by three brick pillars and several pieces of wood which acted as stilts. There were no doors or windows only a roof, otherwise completely open at the front. Below was the kitchen area and I could see a Burmese gentleman, he looked about 75 years of age. He was washing his pots and pans in a bowl. He wore a sarong and straw hat. I walked on a bit just past the stilt houses and the view was breathtaking. An ice blue river was surrounded by bushes and trees. The river narrowed as it neared the point at which I was standing. I felt a lot cooler by just looking at it and was very tempted to climb down and have a paddle, but on second thoughts it would have been a bit dangerous and I did not fancy being stranded on my own in the Far East.

I stood day dreaming for a while and on turning round nearly jumped out of my skin. It was the Burmese man with the sarong and the straw hat. He wore spectacles which seemed very out of place with the rest of his attire and his teeth were black due to chewing 'Beetle Nut'. His smile was the broadest smile I had ever seen. It turned out that what he was interested in was my camera. He was pointing at it so I asked him if I could take his photograph, in the same manner, by pointing at him, and then at my camera. He gave a big nod and took off his hat and a cloth that was wound around the top of his bald head which I suppose gave him more protection from the sun. But by doing this it spoilt the whole way he looked, so I asked him in sign language again, if he would kindly put it back on, which he did. I passed my camera to one of the others as I wanted my photograph taken with him and it was Linda who did the honours. Life was certainly different out here.

I said 'Goodbye' to this old man with all the other Burmese people staring at us as we walked towards the Temple.

As usual on entering the Temple we had to leave our shoes outside, which was very cooling to the soles of the feet as we walked on the marble floors.

Inside it was very grand, full of Buddhist statues and symbols relating to their Religion. Everything was made from gold and precious jewels. The walls were covered with religious murals which were painted very artistically. Brightly painted pictures adorned the walls in beautiful golden frames.

At one side of the temple a man lay asleep on a low wooden bench, lost to the world for a while. Looking on, a monk in an orange sarong was more than likely keeping his eyes on all the treasures.

We waved a last goodbye to these people that stared at us and the coach started up to take us to our last stop of the day which was to visit some hot springs. We were all quite worn out by now, especially the older ones and by the time we arrived at the hot springs we had drunk all the bottles of pop that had been on the coach.

The hot springs looked like swimming pools, but instead of the water being cool it was hot. A garden surrounded the springs with flowers and bushes growing everywhere. I touched the water and it felt quite hot. We were told that anyone wanting to could fry an egg within two minutes.

By the time we had all had a proper look around we were ready for home, which meant the River Kwai Hotel and once again that blue tropical pool.

Tomorrow morning, after paying our last respects at the cemeteries, we would be leaving the Kwai for Hua Hin, which was a small resort on the Gulf of Thailand. We would be there for the remaining four days of our trip, mainly to relax and unwind after our hectic ten days of travelling.

Hua Hin

We all had to be up early this morning as we were leaving the River Kwai Hotel at 8 am. The meaningful part of my trip was now over, but I now possessed knowledge and precious memories of a part of my Dad's life that I did not have before. Although I would have given almost anything for him to have been here with me, it felt good to know that I had fulfilled all the things he had wanted to do and had seen all the sights he had wanted to see. It would have meant a great deal to my Dad if he could have known, that I had been so compelled to do this for him.

Even if the chance to visit the Far East came again, it could never be as wonderful. I had done what I had come to do and the memories I now held would be with me for the rest of my life.

I could not wait to tell my family, especially my Mum about my wonderful adventure, but I had four days to go yet, so would have to make the most of them at Hua Hin.

We had quite a long journey in front of us but to break it, we were going to have a couple of stops. One to have lunch and another to visit a Palace which once belonged to a King Rama and was built in 1858.

Our suitcases were once again being put on the coach and whilst this was being done we had a group 'Kwai Farewell' photograph taken with our Three Pagoda Banner included. Although most of us couldn't wait to get home to tell all our news, it saddened me to think that we may not be able to see one another again. Almost everyone came from different parts of the country, some as far as Scotland and Wales. Only time would tell.

As the coach drove off we all had a last look at the River Kwai Hotel that had been our home for the last four days. I had really enjoyed my stay here and the visits to the prison camp sites had made it much more meaningful.

It was only a few miles to the River Kwai Bridge and Cemeteries. Our first stop was at the Chungkai Cemetery where Pat Heap once again had a few quiet moments at her husband's grave and to say her goodbyes. Although I had not known anyone that had died here at Chungkai, my Dad would have done, so I said my goodbyes for him.

Our next stop was at the River Kwai, where coincidentally, I happened to meet a young girl from Bedford who was working in Thailand for a year, so I took her photograph and promised to take it to her Mum on my return home. It really is a small world.

Before leaving the River Kwai, Linda and I had to have a last walk on the Bridge that our Dads had helped to build. Both of us knowing that we would probably never be here again.

The last stop before our journey to Hua Hin began was to Kanchanaburi Cemetery, where I paid my last respects to Percy Maddams, my brother-in-law's uncle. At least now his family would know where he was and at last could see a photograph of his grave.

Before the coach left I was hoping to see the young Thai artist. My luck was in. He was still at work underneath his large parasol. This time I gave him a souvenir, which was a pen with Bedfordshire, England printed upon it. A very wide smile appeared on his face. We then said our goodbyes, he going back to his painting and I to the coach.

Once out of Bangkok we travelled at a good pace. It was just over a two hour journey to Hua Hin and so far it had already taken us an hour to drive through Bangkok.

We were well into the country now. Seeing, for the last time maybe the Thai scenery through the coach windows. Our first stop was for lunch at a Thai Restaurant. The first thing we saw as the coach stopped was a young elephant outside the entrance to the Restaurant. Everyone was spoiling him by feeding him bananas. We found out his name was Poi and was 2 years old.

The last stop before our arrival at Hua Hin was to see the Palace of King Rama. It was situated on a very high hill, and the only way up was by cable car. It was indeed very grand.

Well, we had finally arrived. Hua Hin was only a small resort but on seeing the Hotel, was completely the opposite. The heat and humidity were even greater than at any of the other places we had visited and I had never before been in such a large luxurious Hotel as this one. There was even a shopping mall.

We were all shown to our rooms. Mine, thankfully on the 3rd floor rather than the 35th. I had a view of the sea and the palm trees running along the length of the beach from my balcony. I would have to make a point of watching the sun rise in the morning.

But for now, I was going to have a look around Hua Hin with some of the others, firstly to buy a few presents for family and friends and secondly to have a good English meal.

That evening we had a couple of drinks in the bar which cost an arm and a leg after which Linda and I went for a late evening walk along the beach with a welcoming breeze to keep us company. It was very tempting to throw off your clothes and run into the water, but there would be plenty of time for that tomorrow. On our way back we could not help but notice the pool area. It was a figure of eight shape with palm trees surrounding it. Now it was time for bed, after first ringing home to make sure everyone was all right and missing me as much as I was missing them.

Rest & Recuperation

My alarm went off purposely at 5.45 am this morning, and I had to wait until 6.15 am before seeing the sunrise. It had been well worth it though, but at the same time I felt quite sad. I had lost count of the times I had wished that my Dad had been here with me. This was one of those times. It was over so very quickly. Suddenly the bright orange-red sun seemed to come up and fill the whole sky with different hues of orange, reds and yellows. One minute it was night, the next day. That is the only way I can describe it.

That afternoon, us younger ones went to the beach with one of the eldest ex-POWs in our group, Jim Hill. He, like us, loved the sea and was going to make the most of it, which we did for a couple of hours. Unfortunately, this was the first and last time for me and Jim, we both got sunburnt. I felt quite ill that night and had to get into a tepid bath to cool my skin after which I covered myself from head to toe with calamine lotion.

Our four days at Hua Hin were much the same. It was good to be able to relax and have more time to talk to each other, discussing how each other felt about all our emotional visits. We also had time, which we had not before, to find out more about each other's personal lives. Most of us were growing very close, and I for one, could not imagine going home and never seeing any of them again.

On our last evening we had a farewell dinner underneath the stars, a meal fit for a Queen.

Now the time was getting closer to going home and I could not wait. I had so much to tell everyone, especially my Mum. I wondered how she would feel hearing and seeing for herself a part of her husband's life she had only been able to imagine.

Going Home

Well, it would not be long now. We were to be at Bangkok Airport around 11.00 pm for take off at midnight – arriving home at Heathrow at 6.00 am on 28th February. Because Thailand is eight hours in front of Greenwich Meantime, the time in England on us boarding the plane would be 6.00 pm – which meant a twelve hour flight.

Until then we all had to while away the time. Some by having a last dip in the pool, others by doing a bit of last minute shopping, if they were lucky enough to have any bahts left. I had just about got rid of mine.

It was a wonderful feeling, to think I would soon be home and I tried to imagine how my Dad, all those years ago would have felt at the thought of home and freedom. It must have been the best feeling in the world for him and for all the other prisoners that had survived their terrible ordeals at the hands of the Japanese.

Once the Japanese realised they were losing the war, Death Marches were brought into force to hide all evidence of brutality. Although it was a terrible shame it had to happen. It was the bombing of Hiroshima and Nagasaki which brought salvation to these prisoners of war. Orders had already been given out from Tokyo to massacre all prisoners once the Allies had mounted an invasion.

Japan, on both occasions, was given the chance to surrender, but refused. Unfortunately, this had been the only way to end the war more quickly saving the lives of men, women and children who were prisoners and who had suffered enough at the hands of the Japanese. Japan after all was the aggressor.

Japan surrendered on 14th August 1945 and throughout the latter half of that month and during September, ex-prisoners began to collect at the ports and airfields of Siam, Malaya and Japan. Men of the 5th Battalion, Beds & Herts Regiment were, in most cases, first taken to India. Some like my father to Rangoon Hospital to recover from their injuries and illnesses and then home, some by air, and others by sea.

For many there was to be no going home, and for many more they were yet to die, the end of the war had come too late for them.

My father chose to go home by sea. This gave him time to put on a bit of weight (most prisoners weighed less than half their normal bodyweight) and to get a bit fitter. It also gave him time to accept in his mind the death of his brother, my uncle.

So, on a cold October day in 1945, my father along with others of the 5th Battalion, Beds & Herts Regiment were home again, almost exactly four years after they had set sail for the Far East. But this time to be welcomed by the cheers of the crowds.

It was now time for us to go home. All our suitcases were waiting to be put on the coach that was to take us to Bangkok Airport. It was just over a two hour journey.

We left the Hotel at 8.00 p.m. to give us plenty of time to get through the traffic and to the Airport. By the time we got there it would be dark.

The plane was an hour late taking off and I hoped that my husband and son would not worry too much about that. It seemed a much longer flight home. I was too excited to sleep and just wanted it to be over. Time went by very slowly but the meals broke the monotony and a chat now and then.

After hours of boredom, the Captain's voice suddenly came over the loudspeaker telling us to fasten our safety belts, that we were nearing Heathrow and that the time was 7.15 a.m. They would be there waiting for us.

We all piled off the plane hugging and kissing each other goodbye and promising to keep in touch, going through the rigmarole of collecting our baggage and piling it onto our trolleys.

Another couple of minutes and I would be with my family.

As soon as I saw their smiling faces tears came to my eyes. I left my trolley and just ran over to them. Even my Mum had got up especially early to come to welcome me home, and that meant a great deal because she was not in very good health and had to take things easy. By now we were all shedding tears. They had known how much this trip had meant to me, especially my Mum, and although no words were said, she knew Dad's dream had been fulfilled and that it was not just me that I had brought home again but part of my Dad as well.

Home & Freedom

On landing my father along with others were taken to transit camps for a few days where further medical checks were carried out before they were able to leave for home.

It was a happy yet sad reunion for him and his parents when he finally walked through that door at 31 Foster Street, as only one of their sons had returned home.

The next and most important thing he had to do was to see Dot, the girl he had left behind four years ago. Her home was at Alfold in Surrey. He had first met her just over a year before he was sent to the Far East, when she had been stationed at Cardington as a LACW in the WAAF. It must have been a wonderful time for them both.

Although my father still was not very fit he went on to be demobbed and settled down to life working as a civil servant at Kempston Barracks, Bedford, the Depot of the Beds & Herts Regiment.

He and Mum married on the 1 June 1946 at Alfold Church in Surrey. As one of Mum's sisters was arranging to be married, it turned out to be a double wedding.

After a honeymoon at Brighton, home, for a while, was with my father's parents until they were lucky enough to rent a Prefab at Elstow in Bedford. My father still suffered from tropical diseases and nightmares but was never one to complain. That I learnt in later years.

Unfortunately, my parents first child, a boy, did not survive. They were planning on calling him Richard after my father's brother who had died as a POW.

On 10th December 1948 I was born, Patricia Ann followed by Brenda Pauline on 1 February 1950. That meant a bigger house was needed, which turned out to be a semi-detached at Hatfield Crescent, on the other side of town.

My sister and I had a wonderful childhood and could not have been happier. Even though Dad was never 100% fit, he was happy with his lot and his family was everything to him. When we were quite small he still used to take part in the part-time Territorial Army and used to go away a couple of times a year for a week or two. I can always remember when it was time for him to come home, looking out for him to appear around the bend at the top of the road. There was no mistaking him in his Army uniform, and even as a four year old, thought he looked so tall and so smart. I would run as fast as I could to meet him, and when I got there he would throw me onto his shoulder with his kitbag on the other, and I knew that inside there would be a present for me and my sister.

I can also remember well the POW Christmas parties we went to and the pub near the Drill Hall, where we went with Mum and Dad, which was called 'the Jungle Arms' by all ex-POWs.

Unfortunately, soon after the mid fifties, Dad had to leave the TA and his job at the Barracks. His health was not good. He had been in hospital with his kidneys and other complaints and had been advised to change his job and do something that would give him more fresh air and exercise. So, he went from working as a civil servant to becoming a milkman, a job which seemed to suit him for some years.

It was in 1967 that his health started deteriorating quite quickly. Although Dad had cancer, none of us really knew before his death. I think he must have known, but he never let on to us and never complained. His heart gave up suddenly at home on 9 July 1968. He was just 53 years of age.

Because of my Dad's early death, he missed out on so much. He never had the pleasure of seeing his daughters marry, or of knowing any of his four grandchildren, of which three are mine: a boy, Steven David George, born on 7th November 1969, a girl, Laura, born on 28th July 1971 and a very welcome latecomer, Gary Walter George born on 9th

November 1984. He would have made such a lovely grandad, but it was not to be – not in this life anyway.

My Trip

My Pilgrimage to Singapore and Thailand was the trip of a lifetime, and other than having had such caring parents and a wonderful family of my own was the next best thing that had happened to me.

It had been the love I still had for my Dad that had taken me all those thousands of miles – a bond that could never be broken, and I now possessed so many wonderful memories of a part of his life that none of us had known much about before. I had always been interested in my Dad's Army life, but the chance of visiting the Far East 'came out of the blue', and I feel very lucky to have been able to do something very special. I am sure that somehow this trip was meant to be and will remember it always.

Since my trip I have had many Reunions with all the friends I made, young and old, with whom I shared so much, and I just hope there will be a great many more.

Compensation & ex-POWs

During my trip I discovered that ex-Far East Prisoners of War were still fighting for an apology and proper compensation, 50 years on, from the Japanese Government.

After all their suffering, an insulting amount of £76 and10 shillings was paid to each Japanese Prisoner of War after the 1951 San Francisco Peace Treaty, with a clause added, which stated that Japan's debt was paid in full. At that time it was all Japan could afford. Now Japan is one of the wealthiest countries in the world and is in a position to shoulder liability and atone for its past.

The following articles appeared at different times in my local paper *The Times & Citizen* in the hope that I might be able to help. People who were prisoners of the Japanese did not only suffer during their captivity, they suffer even now if not physically, mentally or both. A great many Ex-POWs have not even had the chance to visit their comrades graves. That is the least that should be done for them.

It is a known fact that these men, most from the 18th Division who became Prisoners of War of the Japanese were part of the biggest Military disaster in British history, where thousands died so unnecessarily in captivity.

Emotional Singapore trip to visit uncle's grave

Patricia fulfils father's dream

● REUNITED: Patricia pictured at the grave of her uncle in Singapore.

A FATHER'S dream to visit his lost brother's grave has finally been fulfilled by his loving daughter 25 years after his death.

Determined Patricia Bienkowski, 45, of Carrick Road, Bedford, travelled thousands of miles to Singapore and endured scorching heat so she could fulfil her deceased father's dream of visiting his brother's grave.

"It was a very emotional trip – my father always wanted to go back out to see his brother's grave but he never had enough money," Pat said. "If he'd lived I would have been going out there with him but he died 25 years ago and I think his experiences as a prisoner of war contributed to his death."

Patricia returned from her trip to Singapore and Thailand on Monday, February 28, after a two week pilgrimage with ex-servicemen and relatives.

Her father, George Cox, who served with the Beds and Herts Regiment, was captured in 1942 and sent to work on the infamous Burma-Siam 'death-railway.'

Pat's uncle was also a POW in Singapore but never came home as he was killed when his prisoner ship was accidentally bombed by the Americans in 1944.

"I was the first member of my family to ever go out there and see the places my father was held and to visit the grave of my uncle," Pat said. "My mother always wanted to go but she was too ill.

Report by
SIMON BARNES

"I actually walked in my father's foot steps – touched the railway he helped to build.

"I even found the grave of my brother-in-law's uncle at Kanchanaburi cemetery. We knew he had died out there but didn't know if he had a grave or where he was – there wasn't any records.

"We started off in Singapore where they were captured. I saw my uncle's grave at the Kranji war cemetery. After that we went to Changhi prison, where my father was imprisoned in barracks before he was sent to work on different sections of the railway. The POWs dropped like flies out there – they say that for every sleeper on the railway one man died."

Torture

Now Patricia has returned she has brought her family many loving memories and pictures so they can also see something of her father's wartime experiences.

"We couldn't handle the heat out there and yet the POWs had to endure torture along with the heat.

"These soldiers came home with nothing. That is why the publicity is good for them because they are fighting to get compensation.

"I also found four other graves of men from the Beds and Herts Regiment – people may never have seen them."

The names on the four graves are: C.W.Goodwin, J.D.Franklin, T.J.Lee and B.C.Jenkins.

If you know who any of these men were, contact the Herald newsdesk on Bedford 363537.

Pat's war grave visit starts her campaign

A WOMAN who fulfiled her lifetime wish to visit her uncle's war grave has written to the Prime Minister asking for his support with compensation claims for ex-Japanese prisoners of war.

Pat Bienkowski, who was featured in the Herald after she returned from an emotional pilgrimage to Thailand, has written to John Major and North Beds MP Sir Trevor Skeet in support of their compensation claims.

Pat said: "This is a matter of principle and not just compensation. Ever since the end of the war, almost 50 years ago, Japanese prisoners of war have never had any compensation or a public apology.

"No war pension or anything to compensate for the way they were cruelly treated – just a pathetic £50 in the 1950s.

"In the past the Government hasn't fought enough for their men and some have been fighting for compensation themselves.

"Before I went out there I didn't think about it.

Torture

"But since I went and met all the other men who are fighting for this I started to think about what it is they are fighting for.

"Thousands of men died due to the lack of food and water.

"They were allowed one bowl of rice – plus the maggots – a day and dirty water to drink.

This led to disease such as cholera, typhoid or beriberi and if they didn't die of these they died from starvation or torture and beatings."

Report by
SIMON BARNES

Now Pat has received a reply from Sir Trevor Skeet who has promised to forward her letter to the Rt Hon Alistair Goodland MP, and she is eagerly awaiting a reply from John Major.

"There is supposed to be a decision made about this in August," Pat said, "and I have also heard about a group called the Japanese Labour Camp Survivors Association which puts forward claims for compensation to the Ministry of Defence.

"Any ex-Japanese POW or their relatives can put in a claim through this association.

"I hope something is done now, so at least they know that what they went through wasn't, in the end, just forgotten.

"Let's hope the right thing is done for these people now."

Anger at 'snub' from PM Major

ANGRY Pat Bienkowski believes she has been snubbed by the Prime Minister as she bids to get Government backing for her campaign.

Pat from Bedford wrote to both John Major and local MP Sir Trevor Skeet in an attempt to win backing for a campaign to get compensation for ex-POWs from Japanese camps.

But now she has slammed the Government's attitude claiming their letters of reply avoided her questions and fobbed her off.

By SIMON BARNES

Pat said: "I have now received a letter from the Rt Honourable Alastair Goodland, via Sir Trevor Skeet, and a letter from Mr Major's Far East Department evading the whole question of when something will be done.

Cares

"This matter has been going on for 50 years. If the Government cares at all about their men – who suffered at the hands of the Japanese then it is up to them to push the matter, to the forefront now." Pat first became involved in the campaign after an emotional pilgrimage to her uncle's grave in Thailand where he died as a POW.

When she returned Pat was so struck by the extent of the suffering endured by the POWs she decided to see what she could do to help them gain compensation.

"I feel," Pat said, "the Government is waiting for all these people to pop off so that they will be saved a lot of time and trouble.

"There are a lot of Japanese people out there who are also fighting for this cause.

"If the Government doesn't push this they might find themselves being sued by their own people."

Bid to help ex-Japanese POWs to go to The Lords

Pat's campaign gains support

TIRELESS campaigner Pat Bienkowski has finally got the response she has been waiting for from the Government.

Pat started doing her bit to help ex-Japanese prisoners of war gain compensation for their suffering after she returned from an emotional pilgrimage to her uncle's grave in Thailand.

She was so moved by the sights she saw and the accounts she heard from other survivors of the Japanese prisoner of war camp that she decided to take action on her own.

Report by
SIMON BARNES

Since then she has been writing letters demanding action and doing her best to get the campaign publicised to increase support.

Her trip and her efforts on behalf of the ex-POWs have all been covered by the Herald and now clippings from those articles are to be used to support the campaign in the House of Lords.

Pat said: "I received a letter from the Japanese Labour Camp Survivors' Association, who say the matter is to be raised in the House of Lords by their president, Lord Braine. He is going to use my letters to the Foreign Office and cuttings from the Herald as extra ammunition when he raises it.

"I also received a letter from the Foreign and Commonwealth Office, which says the issue is being pushed with the Japanese Government.

"I feel at least something is being done. This is my second letter from the Foreign Office beacause I wasn't satisfied with the first one they sent me. Now at least they have said something is going to be done."

Pat slammed the Government's attitude to ex-POWs last month when she received a letter she claimed avoided her questions and fobbed her off.

Efforts by Pat praised

Report by SIMON BARNES

AFTER MONTHS of tireless campaigning, Pat Bienkowski has received news which has made all her efforts worthwhile.

Pat has been campaigning to help ex-Japanese prisoners of war gain compensation for their suffering since returning from an emotional pilgrimage to her uncle's grave in Thailand.

This week Pat received a letter of thanks for her efforts from the Japanese Labour Camp Survivors' Association and news of their latest decision.

The Association has agreed that six countries are going to take Japan to court for £2.8 billion pounds for slave labour and suffering endured by the POWs.

"I'm only a small part of this," Pat said, "but it's nice to think something is being done. The Government seems to have been turning a deaf ear to all this for fear of losing trade and exports to Japan.

"I intend to keep the ball rolling and I am still writing to the BBC and the papers. This claim might take a long time but the thing is how much time do we have when the average age of the survivors is 75?

"Also, if the Japanese war veterans get £270 a week why does our government pay our war vets nothing? The JLCSA wants to get £10,000 for each POW or widow of a POW.

"This is a matter of principle, its not just about the money. The various companies who used POWs as slave labour during the war are also being pursued."

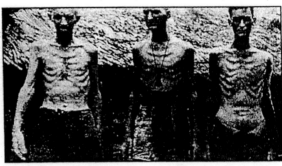

DIED: Compensation comes too late for Mrs Bienkowski's father George Cox, left, and fellow PoWs, above.

'Not too little, but too late'

GOVERNMENT compensation is too late, says a woman whose father suffered hell in a Japanese prisoner of war camp.

Pat Bienkowski, of Carrick Road, Bedford, said it is a shame the men who fought in the Second World War should have waited so long to be acknowledged.

She said: "I'm very pleased it has happened, but they still haven't received an apology from the Japanese government. And it's sad so many have died before being recognised by their own Government.

"For all these years they have been swept under the carpet. They were used as slaves out there, so many were killed and now a lot of the survivors are dead.

"I don't think the Government wanted to do this, I think they did it because of public pressure. They don't want to upset the Japanese because we do a lot of trade with them, but our men fought and died for their country. They should have been the first consideration."

Mid Beds MP Jonathan Sayeed said: "I have spent a great deal of time lobbying the Government. My own uncle, a captain in the gunners, died in Changi."

EPILOGUE

Since first writing this book, ex-POWs of the Japanese or their widows will have received £10,000 in the form of a Special Gratuity from the British Government for their pain and suffering during captivity. They had the support of The Japanese Labour Camp Survivors Association and The Royal British Legion for this, and finally the Government agreed that all ex POWs living or their widows get the recognition they so rightly deserve.

The Canadian and Isle of Man ex-POWs of the Japanese had recently been granted compensation from their Governments and I feel this forced the hand of the British Government to at last do the same. It is just a great pity that most POWs are not here to receive the recognition they so rightly deserved, and also a great pity that the Japanese Government could not bring themselves to do the right thing.

In 1997 a new Charity was founded. 'Children and Families of Far East Prisoners of War', of which I am a member.

The Charity's main aim is to have built an Educational Centre (maybe at Duxford in Cambridge) which will tell the story of British Servicemen who served and/or died out in the Far East under captivity during 1942-45.

There will be the names, ranks, and numbers of all men from the different Regiments who served out in the Far East. There will be maps, photographs etc. The building will be a lasting memorial to all of them, be they husbands, fathers, sons, uncles or brothers, and we will know that the hell they went through as Prisoners of War will never be forgotten.

Since becoming a member of COFEPOW I have met many interesting people and have had the pleasure of helping to arrange on behalf of COFEPOW a very special service and tree planting dedicated to all FEPOWs. This was held on 13th Feb 2000 at Elstow Abbey Church, Elstow, in Bedford. The tree was planted by H.M. Lord Lieutenant Samuel Whitbread and the Service conducted by Rev. Richard Huband. There were Standard Bearers from the Royal British Legion, Burma Star and the Bedfordshire and Hertfordshire Regiment.

Mr Terry Waite CBE and Air Marshal Sir John Baird (Patrons of COFEPOW) also attended. A memorial stone dedicated to all FEPOWs sits under the tree in the Churchyard. It was a most memorable day for me and I hope there will be many others.

At least 50% of any profits I receive from the sale of this book will go to The C.O.F.E.P.O.W. Memorial Fund.

Patricia Bienkowski

Wherever we went in Thailand we received a warm welcome. Members of the Three Pagodas Ex-POW Group are photographed here at the Pitman restaurant in Bangkok.

The Three Pagodas Pass at the border between Thailand and Burma.

Underground bunkers at Fort Canning, Singapore.

Two of the original cattle wagons that transported POWs from Singapore to Thailand during World War II.

Changi Gaol in Singapore, where my father was a prisoner in World War II.

The chapel in the grounds at Changi prison, Singapore -- a replica of the one built by POWs during the war.

The entrance to Chungkai war cemetery, Thailand.

Chungkai war cemetery, Thailand.

The grave of Percy Maddams at Kanchanaburi cemetery, Thailand.

The author, lays a wreath on the grave of Percy Maddams (her brother-in-law's uncle) at Kanchanaburi cemetery, Thailand. The wartime prison camp was nearby.

The memorial walls at Kranji cemetery, Singapore.

Kranji cemetery, Singapore.

The author finds her uncle's name on the memorial walls at Kranji cemetery, Singapore and lays some flowers for him.

The author, standing on the River Kwai bridge, Thailand.

The author, with fellow members of the three pagodas ex-POW group taking refreshment at a riverside cafe with the River Kwai bridge in the background.